LAUGHING AT THE SUN

The Story of a Man Who

Changed His Spots

- A MEMOIR -

MICHAEL NEJMAN

D1372336

THIRD ACT PRESS

LAUGHING AT THE SUN – The Story of the Man Who Changed His Spots

Michael Nejman

ISBN-10:1512080977
ISBN-13: 978-1512080971

Library of Congress Control Number: 2015907602

CreateSpace Independent Publishing Platform, North Charleston, SC

This book is based on true events. The conversations in the book all come from the author's recollections, though they are not written to represent word-for-word transcripts. Rather, the author has retold them in a way that evokes the feeling and meaning of what was said; and in all instances, the essence of the dialogue is accurate. In one case, in order to maintain the anonymity of a former romantic partner, the author has changed her name and a few identifying details.

The poems "Intimacy" and "Mysterious Ways" by Edward Proffitt are used with permission by the author's surviving partner, Robert Fischer.

This book is dedicated to
all of the romantic partners
who I made mistakes with,
in preparation for getting it right
for the love of my life, Laura

ACKNOWLEDGMENTS

In 1997 I went through a mid-life crisis and thanks to the friendship and guidance of Bob Fischer and Michael Kardas, I got through it successfully. I was told that a leopard can't change his spots, however I'm living proof that it can be done.

In 2005, I met Laura and I am forever grateful.

In completing this book, I have deeply felt gratitude for Michael Held for all of his friendship, support, positivity and technical savvy. I am also so very thankful for Barbara and Jeff Pietroski, Judith Barahal, Amanda Nielsen and Deborah Abbott for their invaluable editorial guidance, support and feedback. I also appreciate Vicki Atkinson, Karen Johnstone and Karen Freese for their feedback.

In addition, I am very thankful for Mary O'Donohue for her helpful insights, coaching and feedback.

David Henry Sterry and Arielle Eckstut of *The Book Doctors* helped develop my pitch, which assisted me in thinking about how to market this book.

Mike McCandless was instrumental for informing me about self-publishing through his Publish It Yourself class in the Continuing Education Department of Harper College.

Great music - and a rare radio station that offers it - helped my writing process and made my life more enjoyable for the past few decades. A big thanks to Chicago's WXRT, their program director Norm Winer, and the best deejays in the business — Terri Hemmert, Lin Brehmer and Tom Marker — who are synonymous with the station.

I would also be remiss if I didn't thank Oprah Winfrey for introducing me to gratitude diaries many years ago. I wasn't a

regular viewer of her show, however I had an uncanny ability to catch episodes that would eventually impact my life. Learning about gratitude diaries, and keeping one, really helped me get through my mid-life crisis.

Finally, I couldn't have written this book without the unconditional love, patience, understanding and support provided by the love of my life, Laura.

LAUGHING AT THE SUN

Chapter One

My sudden desire to kill him might seem outrageous, however it shouldn't be too surprising...

"*Writing,*" Bob Fischer scoffed. "I can't think of a more impotent act."

He paused for dramatic effect, allowing his words to saturate the air.

"Nobody *reads* anymore," he continued with the conviction of an older brother cruelly setting his younger sibling straight on the existence of Santa Claus. He was walking slightly behind me as we carefully navigated the canyon edge along the trail.

Fair enough, I thought. Not the greatest last words to breathe before leaving this world, but better than some. I had just reminded him of how much I wanted to be a writer and he reminded me of what a jerk he can be at times. His remarks sounded much like the faultfinding voice that often resides in my head, critiquing my every goal and dream. My first impulse, admittedly a hasty one, was to push him over the nearby ledge and into the canyon, an immediate solution that would

promptly end his antagonistic commentary and thus soothe my throbbing headache. But there were laws about such actions in Utah and I needed to take a deep breath and pause before I did something foolish. For now, such an action would need to remain a fantasy, a daydream designed to help me cope with Mr. Sunshine.

Focus on the natural beauty before me, I thought. I looked out over the canyon and admired the constantly changing red and orange hues of the rocks as shadows from clouds above flowed over them, providing a kinetic light show. Soak in the grandeur of nature; block out Bob's negativity. *Soak in nature, block out negativity,* I silently chanted. The pulsing pain in my head began to subside and my breathing shifted from tight, shallow breaths to those more deep and cleansing. I was in the moment, fully enjoying the setting and my opportunity to appreciate this incredible view. I stared at the canyon with great intensity, burning the image into my memory so that I could retrieve it for future enjoyment during those bland, dreary days to come when I'd be tethered to my desk back in my office. *Life is good,* the voice in my mind declared, *and I am a lucky man to experience this moment.*

"When can we fucking leave?" Bob said abruptly with a deep nasal whine, invading my Zen moment like a squad of Imperial Stormtroopers breaking up a Rebel Alliance kegger.

My next move was spontaneous and fluid, emotional and angry. I grabbed Bob by the collar of his shirt, crushing fabric within my tight grasp, and then pushed him just beyond the trail's edge. His toes were on terra firma, his heels unsupported by the ground. Only my ten fingers clenching his collar were keeping him from plunging more than 300-feet over the cliff. We were face-to-face, so I could see the panic in his eyes.

"I'm going to throw you into the motherfucking canyon!" I declared, apparently with considerable volume as I sensed many of the tourists around us stopping their conversations and photo taking to observe Bob's predicament.

The canyon's updraft provided a slight breeze that tickled the hair on my legs and then traveled up into my hiking shorts.

This sensation caused me to pause, take a very deep breath, and contemplate my next move.

For the first time all day, he was silent.

Today was Day Three of a road trip with an expiration date that maxed out 24 hours earlier; a road trip that just ten days earlier had seemed like an excellent chance to have some fun with my buddy while sorting out a few personal problems. But now it appeared that our westward excursion had taken a wrong turn, and we were on one heck of a rocky road and heading for this cliff. I had grown tired of his steady stream of sarcasm, criticism and cynicism. Not that he wasn't right most of the time, but that just made his commentary all the more unbearable to hear. Hell, I realized I was often in denial, but an honest assessment of my particular situation wasn't necessarily what I wanted to hear. I just wanted a supportive reaction from a friend, confirmation that I had made the right decision regarding The Big Break-Up with Jennifer. And I was confused. Really confused. Not only with my own personal crisis with Jennifer, but Bob — my best friend for nearly 15 years and a married man and father of three — had just come out six months earlier saying he wanted to be with Edward instead of his wife Paula.

This transition may have been on his mind for a long time, but for me it was a new reality that wasn't easy to grasp. I suppose I should have known Bob was gay all along. There were signs, although a lack of gaydar rendered me clueless most of the time. For instance, he tended to wear gaudy costume jewelry, which I assumed was just part of his eccentric, flamboyant artist façade. Besides, there had been plenty of rock stars that wore jewelry — and even make-up — and they were chick-magnets; no need to question their sexual orientation.

Also, Bob went clubbing almost exclusively at gay nightspots, yet that never struck me as surprising since these establishments consistently had the most interesting crowds and the best dance music. It was not unusual to see gays, straights and everyone else on the sexual orientation spectrum

sharing the dance floor and gyrating, drinking and sweating into the early morning hours.

Above all though, Bob always offered the best advice when it came to dealing with my relationship problems. He was a masculine Dear Abby personified, my go-to guy when it came to questions about intimacy, romance and maintaining relationships. The rub was this: although his insightful input was invariably helpful, he was hardly a good role model, often exhibiting selfish behavior incongruous to his counsel. The old adage, "Do as I say, not as I do," would come to mind.

After a nearly 15-year friendship — a friendship where we had shared a lot of life experiences together — I thought that I knew him; however, it became painfully obvious that that this wasn't the case. As a result I felt betrayed, lied to, and marginalized. Didn't he trust that I would have supported him no matter what? Who was I to judge? I had an open mind and, most importantly, I was his friend.

Writing is an impotent act. The gist of his words, shrewdly designed to undermine my desire and confidence to become a writer, was the spark that ignited this Molotov cocktail of my growing frustration. My incendiary reaction was the result of his on-going nagging, impatience and self-centered need to get back into the vehicle and quickly on to our destination, stopping only for physiological needs such as restrooms, repose, and life-supporting nourishment, nothing more. Bob's insensitive comment, combined with his whiny, childish antics from earlier in the day, had taken me to this explosive breaking point.

My sudden desire to kill him might seem outrageous, however it shouldn't be too surprising as he was my best friend, one I loved like a brother. And, as best friends and siblings often do, he sometimes exploited my weaknesses and playfully harassed me in a constant and twisted game to get a rise out of me. A paradox for sure, but hardly a shocking development. But this time, he had sorely underestimated my tolerance for his boorish behavior. This time he had gone too

far. I needed to stand up to him, confront his bullying, and declare my boundaries for such antics.

"You lied to me!" I said and gritted my teeth. The sun made me squint, so my delivery was reminiscent of Clint Eastwood in an early spaghetti western.

Bob looked at me and then down at my fists clenching his shirt, where a rush of adrenaline caused my hands to shake slightly. Then, he looked to the side and over his shoulder at the floor of the canyon, a drop that would require a series of pinball-like bounces before hitting the bottom.

Bob saw his future and he gulped.

Chapter Two

A Road Scholar on a Quest

Ten days earlier.

Freedom. For me, freedom meant the open road, a tankful of gas, a mix-tape of good music and a warm summer's day. The destination needed to be exotic in nature, and by my Midwestern standards that meant domestic places linked to adventure and fun, like Yellowstone, the Rockies, or California. I embraced romantic notions of the open road, what Norman Bel Geddes referred to as "the Magic Motorways," with strains of Bruce Springsteen's epic "Born to Run" playing in the soundtrack of my mind. Like Sal Paradise and Dean Moriarty in Jack Kerouac's classic novel *On the Road*, and Captain America and Billy in the movie *Easy Rider*, I longed for free-spirited cross-country travel as a Road Scholar on a quest for kicks, along with time to contemplate the state of my life.

The phone call came as a surprise.

"You want to drive to Palm Springs with me?" This was a typical beginning for a phone conversation with Bob Fischer. No greeting. No prelude. Just a direct question that was usually quite out-of-the-ordinary. He continued after a slight pause with an ironic statement meant to entice me with his offbeat humor, "It's God's Waiting Room." This was a reference to the countless retirees residing in the area, living out their final days.

He added, "Just think, it'll get you away from those boring suburbs." Although this last statement was a general criticism about living in a sleepy suburban community, it was more of a direct dig against my choice to live in one.

After another pause, he said, "I'll take care of your expenses and fly you home." Yet, another pause, and then, "Michael, my Polish pal, you there? You up for a road trip or what?"

It was May 1997, an era of certain electronic and technological deficiencies. Road travel was somewhat primitive. There was no MapQuest or GPS. No comforting female voice to tell us where to turn as she recalculated our last wrong move. We just had a *Rand McNally Road Atlas*, the Bible of the Open Road, and a sincere hope that the road construction gods would smile gently upon our journey. Since I lived near Chicago, his proposal meant a trip of approximately 2,000 miles.

Bob's call also came at a time when I was at a crossroads in my life having reached three milestones earlier that year: I had just turned 40, realized 15 years at my job, and attained almost six years in a romantic relationship, although at the moment we were living apart.

My delusional self would say that life was good: I had matured, sustained a stable career and found the partner of my dreams. Embracing total denial, I would further assess these milestones not only as progress in my life, but grand accomplishments, life goals of which to be proud.

Recently, however, I encountered a moment of clarity that

dashed my fantasy. It came, as many do, in the middle of the night when the noise of the day was stifled and one could think clearly.

As I lay in bed, in total darkness, I began to realize that two of the three milestones were situations that were not all that positive, and in fact, much nearer the Crisis Stage than not.

I had indeed turned 40, what many would undeniably accept as *middle-age*. Well, middle-age if one is lucky enough to survive eight decades. One statistic I had seen for the average life expectancy for a white male in the United States was 76.5 years, which would indicate that I had already arrived north of middle-age. When it came to aging, I had hoped to be well *above average*, but that achievement was still to be determined.

As for my job, I had worked at a college for 15 years, but I felt unfulfilled and unsure of my future. I felt lost. Was life passing me by? Did I lose sight of what I truly wanted to achieve in my career? As a young man I might not have had a clear vision for my future, but had I known what awaited me at 40, I would have been unimpressed and disappointed.

And then there was my relationship with Jennifer that had recently come to an end. She had suggested I move out. And I did. This was not a new occurrence in my life. Since my divorce in 1980, I had a lengthy string of unsuccessful relationships.

I had just left one of the great loves of my life —— my muse and someone who had helped me achieve several important life goals. And each day I struggled with my decision. Was I right to move on, or should I turn around and fight for someone I could still make a life with? This question haunted me, and it was one I needed to contemplate and resolve in a manner I could fully accept. I didn't want my future contaminated with more of the *what ifs* of regret.

A road trip might be just what I needed to get away from my daily routine and take time to reflect on my life and ponder several tough decisions. Having gotten to middle-age, I found decision-making much more stressful. Now there was less time left to correct potential mistakes and live the life I wanted, the life I deserved. I needed to make good decisions, the *right* decisions for me. As Leon Russell had shared in a lyric, "How many days has it been since I was born, how many days until I die?" Where was I at on my personal timeline? Was I closer to the beginning or the end?

All of these thoughts raced through my mind as I continued my phone conversation with Bob.

"This is kind of sudden. What's the deal? Are we on the run?" Bob was very spontaneous, so his sudden desire for a road trip wasn't necessarily suspect. Yet, I felt a need for additional information.

"No, nothing like that," Bob replied quickly. After a pause, he added mysteriously, "We'll be transporting *some goods*."

Be cautious, I thought. *Get more information.*

"Define 'goods.' Legal or illegal?"

"ART," he shouted into the phone. "MY art," he declared with the cheesy swagger of a TV pitchman. I could imagine him snickering to himself. He continued, "I've got a truckload of my paintings that I need to get home. They've been in storage long enough."

Bob, an artist, had moved from Chicago to Los Angeles five years earlier in 1992 with his wife and three children. Now he was living in a resort-like home in Palm Springs with his new partner Edward. A significant stash of his sizeable, color-filled canvases had been safely secured in a storage unit in Chicago. Many of the paintings had been on exhibit at a gallery show of his work several months earlier. It was now time to transport them west.

An image of Bob and me selling his artwork at truck stops or along the side the road crossed my mind. A hand-painted banner nearby declaring: "Starving Artist Sale! All paintings must go! 100% acrylic! If you have space above your sofa, we can fill it!"

This adventure sounded alluring, yet being very conscious of time, I asked, "So, how long will it take?"

"If we could leave next Monday, that would be perfect."

I quickly calculated that I had about a week to get clearance for the time off from my boss. Since I worked at a college and it was after the end of the spring semester, it was an especially good time to take a week or two off. This road trip idea was starting to sound very promising.

"I'm interested," I said cautiously. "But are we going pedal-to-the-metal or a more laidback pace?" I had driven cross-country a couple of times before, once with an extreme time limit that required long shifts behind the wheel, and another more leisurely. "I'm all for a trip that allows for bathroom breaks, hot showers, and taking time for a few Kodak Moments at points of interest along the way."

"I'm thinking a week."

"A five-day or seven-day week?"

"*Oy*, enough with the fucking questions. Five. Six travel days tops!" he assured me. "You'll have plenty of time for Kodak Moments and stops along the way. And of course you're welcome to stay at the house a few days. Afterward, you can go see your sister, or L.A., and then fly back whenever." My younger sister and her family had lived in Rancho Cucamonga, not far from Palm Springs, since the late '70s, and I made it a goal to see her every year or two. A visit was long overdue.

I assessed the situation: spontaneous adventure on the open road, my expenses covered, and quality time with my best friend. What could go wrong?

I often prided myself on making decisions quickly, relying on my intuition, my gut reaction. I replied, "I'm in!"

Bob's proposal sounded like fun and it would give us some time together, something we didn't share much of since his move to the West Coast. When he lived in Chicago, we got together weekly. Now, there were only phone calls and perhaps an annual visit. More importantly though, I felt this trip would provide me with some quality time for reflection to plan the next move in my life.

There was one caveat I needed to share with Bob, "Provided I can get the time away from the office, of course.

Give me a day to work it out."

"Alright, I'll check back with you in a day or so. Lots to do, gotta go!"

His last statement was punctuated with a click, and the sudden end of our phone connection. Just like a hyper hummingbird on a nectar mission, he appeared, hovered for a moment, and then, was gone in an instant.

"Take care," I said out loud to no one, feeling a need for closure. As I hung up, I suddenly got a sick feeling in my stomach. Bob and I were great friends living in separate residences with plenty of room to buffer our differences, but what would it be like in a small truck cabin and sharing cramped hotel rooms? I couldn't help but wonder if this was a decision I would soon regret.

Chapter Three

Chicago's Odd Couple

A born and bred Chicagoan, Bob was an established artist well before he had transplanted himself to California in 1992, after a session with a fortuneteller encouraged the move. He was an eccentric, bohemian, Jewish artist, who until recently was a married father of three. I, on the other hand, was a divorced, athletic, fun-loving but somewhat uptight ——at least by Bob's standards — slightly neurotic former altar boy who struggled with making commitments.

My marriage to my high school sweetheart, Candy, had established a negative relationship template I adopted for the next 15 years. I thought our marriage was forever love, only to find out that she preferred her girlfriend. We were divorced before we reached our second wedding anniversary. To fans of the TV show *Friends*, it might have been known as The Ross Syndrome. This heart-breaking result dashed my belief in the chance of having a committed, permanent romantic relationship, so I got close to my successive love interests, yet remained emotionally unavailable. Using this tactic I could avoid future love-related tragedy; however, it left a long, messy trail of failed relationships.

At a glance, Bob and I were a 1990s version of Oscar and Felix from *The Odd Couple* fame, although the stereotypes were slightly modified. Bob was a gay artist with Oscar's sloppy habits, relaxed hygiene, and desire to wear whatever came into view from the closet — or floor — that morning, while I was athletic and straight, with all of Felix's fastidious habits and grooming. I had just turned 40, while Bob was eight years older. I reached six-foot-one, while Bob fell a full head shorter. At a glance, people often mistook me for *Dirty Dancing* Patrick Swayze, while Bob had a "Walk On the Wild Side" Lou Reed urban-chic appearance.

Regardless of our differences, we laughed a lot and enjoyed each other's company. At times, I would describe our friendship as the epitome of a love/hate relationship, or perhaps to be more accurate love/annoyed. We certainly had our highs and lows, yet we were best buddies

When I first met Bob in the early 1980s, he was quite a bit heavier, with a full-beard, which made him look like Francis Ford Coppola during the *Apocalypse Now* shoot. Even though he was less than average height, his bulky size gave him far more presence. Now, as we prepared to go on our westward adventure, he had trimmed down to an athletic, almost svelte physique, which made him look more young and virile. Bob looked the role of the contemporary, post-modern *artiste* in short-cropped spiky hair, round-rimmed tinted glasses, and with slight stubble on his cheeks and chin, along with an urban, paint-splattered bohemian wardrobe.

Back in the mid-'90s, he typically dressed in Fischer-chic: a black leotard, yellow running shorts adorned with *Batman* logos, bright gold hand-painted leather gym shoes with bold red laces, mismatched fluorescent socks and a leather coat with a dramatic image of the Doors' rock icon Jim Morrison painted on the back. Bob's attire not only attracted attention, *it demanded it!* The Gatekeepers of Fashion would have certainly given him high marks for creativity and style, while the Fashion

Police would have arrested him for impersonating an eccentric homeless guy.

Sans leather jacket, one's attention was immediately drawn to the tattoo of the 1930s tragic Hollywood actress Frances Farmer, Fischer's signature image, on his right bicep. He often wore enough garish costume jewelry to look like a drag queen's fairy godfather, and his glasses could have been borrowed from Elton John during his more flamboyant phase.

"My greatest fear in life is being boring," he once told me. Adjectives describing Bob Fischer and his artwork have included provocative, pop, erotic, eccentric, electric and eclectic; but boring his art was not.

Fischer had been hailed as "The Windy City Warhol" by *People* magazine and he had a rich and diversified Arts background that ranged from staging elaborate neo-vaudevillian performance art events with special themes, to painting on canvas, clothing, furniture, and directly on people. His vibrant, colorful images were often of pop celebrity icons Elvis, Madonna and Marilyn Monroe, as well as early Hollywood stars Marlene Dietrich, Judy Garland, Tallulah Bankhead, Cecil Beaton and Harpo Marx. Bob was also known to capture on canvas graphic, scintillating sex scenes showcasing lurid, leather-bound, sadomasochistic partners, brash drag queens, and world-weary, tattooed strippers.

His vivid fashion sense and glaring style certainly held a place in sophisticated urban settings where he might draw only slight attention from pedestrians as he walked down the sidewalk. Nevertheless, this is might not be true of the small, Middle-American towns off Interstate 80 exits, one of our routes to Palm Springs, where he would attract the kind of attention that could be dangerous to our physical health. When traveling, I think it's best to blend in with the locals to avoid looking like a tourist, or worst still, a flamboyant artist making a fashion statement with accessories secured from a trashy retro resale shop.

This concern of mine led to a rather frank phone call to Bob one evening, a few days before we were to embark on our trip.

"Have you ever seen the movie *Deliverance*, Bob?"

"Yeah, why?"

"Now I know we're not going to the deep South where rednecks might take offense to your wardrobe, but I think it might be best if you," I paused for a second to think of the best way to continue. "*Toned down* a bit. You know, maybe leave your silver and leather bracelet, the one with the rhinestones, at home for instance."

There was a pregnant pause on the other end of the phone conversation.

"I get your point," Bob said in full agreement and he was hummingbird gone.

Click!

Chapter Four

The Most Critical Component of a Road Trip

The next few days were a blur as I secured the vacation time from work, packed a couple of week's worth of clothes, emptied the fridge of contents sure to spoil, tossed all the garbage (one does not want to return to a foul-smelling apartment), arranged to stop my mail, and paid bills that were due before my return.

Thanks to my highly developed organizational skills and laser-like focus, I was then able to quickly complete the majority of tasks at hand, allowing plenty of time to address what I sincerely felt was the most critical component of a road trip: Music.

A good mix-tape, or two, would be essential for a successful outing.

It's difficult now to appreciate the challenge I faced. In 1997, the pre-digital age didn't have playback devices capable of containing thousands of songs, or streaming services providing endless options. Space was limited. Decisions needed to be made, and time was of the essence.

Some people were really anal and meticulous about their

mix-tapes and the selection of tracks for the perfect sound-travel experience. I didn't think I was as particular as some of them. I didn't worry about chronological order, or the hit status of the record. That is, some people only focused on the Top 40 hits. I preferred the Deep Cuts, songs that hadn't been over-played on Top 40 and Oldies radio stations. Led Zeppelin was a perfect example. I couldn't tolerate listening to "Stairway to Heaven," played ad nauseam on the airwaves as well as my turntable, for decades, although I'd be delighted with the lesser played, "Ramble On" (plus, it dealt with traveling, which made it thematic).

Of course, I didn't want to get too hung up on theme. I was developing a road trip tape, but I didn't want to limit myself to songs with only travel in their core. I was also interested in songs that just sounded good as one cruised down the highway. Dynamics were also important. One needed to stay awake, so adrenaline-pumping cuts were essential to make up for caffeine-deprived segments on the road. Yet, we also needed mellower tunes that simply had a good vibe, so we could maintain our alertness without burning out on ever-building-but-never-climaxing Extreme Hard Rock. There needed to be good pacing and timing. A cassette tape was 90-minutes long (120-minute tapes often jammed, so I preferred cassette tapes of a shorter length), which meant 45 minutes per side (it sucked to split songs between sides, which is probably why 8-track tapes faded away with their four disruptive jumps per tape).

To a musical Philistine, selecting appropriate cuts would be a simple process of determining which ear candy to string together – without rhyme, reason or substance for making one's decisions. But for true Audio Architects, who relished in the competitive goal of determining the ultimate travel mix for a cross-country road trip, there would be an intense critical struggle to contend with while going through the process. For me, the Rolling Stones' *Exile on Main Street* was *the* definitive rock album of all time. End of story. Also most, if not all of the songs on this double-album, were perfect for the open road. In fact, I would argue that *Exile* is a "Desert Island Album." It's an essential album (or in this case, double-album) that one should have if ever shipwrecked on a deserted island with only a few records to play – provided of course, that one had washed up on shore with a turntable and a power source. Thus, I decided to simply bring *Exile* on cassette and not stress out on the almost inconceivable process of determining its "best cuts."

Yet before I continued, I needed to take a moment to put my critic's ear and ego in check. I had to avoid being a hardcore music aficionado and not try to make a statement by selecting only songs with cool status. I didn't want to get too hung up on the latest, greatest *fave raves* on my turntable, showing off a knack I have for selecting the Next Big Thing by choosing little-known bands on the cusp of discovery. I needed to be sensitive to my travel partner's needs, too, and not create a complex, sophisticated mix that would result in countless questions like "who's this band?" and "where did you find this?" On the other side of the musical spectrum, I also wanted to make sure I wasn't selecting only Classic Rock cuts as well as vanilla, mainstream music often embraced by Request Radio deejays on Oldies stations.

Time was limited, so I grabbed a yellow legal pad of paper and jotted down songs I immediately associated with the open road from my personal library of albums and cassette tapes:

- Bruce Springsteen's "Born to Run" (of course!)
- Steppenwolf's "Magic Carpet Ride"
- Chuck Berry's "Route 66"
- Golden Earring's "Radar Love"
- Joe Walsh's "Rocky Mountain Way"
- Jimi Hendrix's "Crosstown Traffic"
- Tom Petty's "Running Down a Dream"
- War's "Low Rider"
- Allman Brothers' "Ramblin' Man"

- The Eagles' "Take it Easy"
- Simon & Garfunkel's "America"

These were mostly songs from the 1960s and 1970s, songs of my youth, songs that conjured up images of sun, fun, fast cars and half-baked joints.

Then, I started a list of adrenaline-injected songs that were great to crank up with the car windows down:

- Iggy Pop's "Lust for Life" (my battle-cry for living back in those days) and "Five Foot One"
- Van Halen's version of the Kinks' classic, "You Really Got Me"
- Mountain's "Mississippi Queen"
- ZZ Top's "La Grange"
- The Cure's "Never Enough"
- INXS's "Suicide Blonde"
- The Cult's "She Sells Sanctuary"
- Lenny Kravitz's "Bring it On"
- Aerosmith's "Love in an Elevator"
- AC/DC's "Back in Black" and "Highway to Hell"
- Anything off of Nirvana's *Nevermind* album

Finally, I wanted songs with a good "smooth cruise" vibe:

- Fine Young Cannibals' "Good Thing"
- James' "Born of Frustration"
- Blur's "There's No Other Way"
- Replacements' "Someone Take the Wheel"
- Anything off of the *Greatest Hits* album from Tom Petty and the Heartbreakers and Los Lobos' *Kiko* album

What an overwhelming selection of choices! I felt like Meryl Streep in *Sophie's Choice* having to (spoiler alert!) choose between my children. Of the titles I jotted down, I pulled together what I felt was a solid mix for a 90-minute tape. I also grabbed pre-recorded tapes of the Stones' *Exile,* Nirvana's *Nevermind,* Los Lobos' *Kiko* and Tom Petty and The Heartbreakers' *Greatest Hits.* Audio ecstasy! I started to feel better about the impending cross-country escapade I would embark on with Bob, although I also began to pray he'd forget to bring his disco tapes.

Chapter Five

Day One on the Road:
Schaumburg, Illinois to Omaha, Nebraska

Bob was scheduled to pick me up on Saturday, May 24, at 10:30 a.m. at my apartment complex in Schaumburg, Illinois. The location was very near Route 53, the beginning of our California-bound adventure. I got up at 6 a.m. and made sure I had plenty of time to shower, shave, eat breakfast, finish packing and tend to a lengthy checklist of last-minute details before leaving my second-floor studio for an extended amount of time.

The night before, I had placed my medium-sized duffel bag, packed and ready (minus my faux leather toiletries bag) within inches of my front door, as if I might forget to bring it with had it been placed anywhere else.

It was still dark in my apartment when my alarm sounded and I leapt out of bed. Actually, I was up an hour prior to the alarm, ticking away my "things to do" list in my head, making sure every detail was examined and settled. My shower that morning was much longer than the normal, highly efficient five-minute scrub-and-rinse cycle I practiced most days. Just in case we decided to drive an extra-long first shift, making sure we got through the tedious flatland states, I wanted to make sure I was prepped and clean for the day. I rinsed off, turned off the water, and then grabbed a towel to dry off my torso and limbs.

Turning on the transistor radio near the bathroom sink, I listened to the news radio traffic and weather reports as I brushed back my wet hair, lathered up my cheeks and chin, and shaved. According to the news announcer it was 6:30 a.m., time for my breakfast: an apple, bowl of cereal, wheat toast lightly buttered, and a four-ounce glass of orange juice. While I ate, I watched my small, portable TV, catching the local news and weather forecast, again checking on traffic, which on a Saturday was non-existent. All was well.

By 7 a.m., I went through my mental checklist and my "leaving the apartment for vacation" ritual of making sure windows were closed and latched, dishes were all washed and tucked away, garbage was all sent down the chute at the end of the hallway, and the place was tidy for my return. I blow-dried my hair, dressed in my khaki shorts, black T-shirt, and gym shoes, all laid out the night before, and flossed and brushed my teeth twice. I packed my toiletries to make sure I had aspirin, vitamins, Pepto Bismol tablets, contact cleaner and solution, dental floss, a toothbrush with holder, a couple of small toothpaste tubes, hairbrush, and fingernail clippers. Then I tucked the toiletries into my duffel bag, next to two plastic-wrapped yellow Kodak disposable cameras with 36 exposures each. If I stayed frugal, the 72 images would adequately document our trip.

I loved the process of preparation. I think that was why I was so good at my job as a producer of cultural events and activities at a nearby college; I not only developed a Plan A and Plan B, but also Plans C, D, and E. I hated surprises, and since I had little control as to how an event might unroll on any given day, I made sure I could identify a successful solution to a problem as quickly as possible.

I glanced at my wristwatch. It was only 8 a.m.! I had more than two hours before Bob would arrive. I pulled out the spiral notebook I had bought for the journey to use as a journal. On the first page, I created a make-shift calendar. I simply listed the dates and days, one on each line: May 24, Saturday; May 25, Sunday; May 26, Monday; and so on. I could jot down each day's destination, and perhaps, our mileage and trip highlights. On page two, I wrote down a few thoughts about my goal for the trip and what I hoped to accomplish along the way. In the back of the journal, I recorded names, phone numbers and directions to friends and family in the Los Angeles/Palm Springs area that I intended to visit while I was in town. My two sisters, for instance, one living in Rancho Cucamonga and the other in Mission Viejo; and an agent or two who I had met through my job at Harper College to see if they'd like to have lunch or grab a drink. One name I had written prominently on the first back page was Jackie Miller. Recently, I had co-produced an event at Harper with Zanies Comedy Club owner, Rick Uchwat, featuring comedian Bill Maher; Miller was his agent. She was one of the nicest agents I've ever worked with, and she promised to secure studio tickets for me to see Maher's controversial and very funny TV show, *Politically Incorrect*. I had tentatively planned on getting to L.A. by May 29 or 30, and luckily they were taping the show that week.

I really enjoyed going to TV talk show tapings and made personal goals of seeing my favorite late-night hosts. My personal highlights included: *The Tonight Show with Johnny Carson* (along with Ed McMahon and Doc Severenson; a rare treat to see all three on the same show with their vacation schedules!), Jay Leno subbing for Carson on *The Tonight Show*; I sat in the Dog Pound on the *Arsenio Hall Show*; and I had seen David Letterman both at NBC (for my 30th birthday), and at the Ed Sullivan Theater when he later moved to CBS. I couldn't wait to go see Maher in action and wondered who his guests might be. As I finished compiling my mini-directory in the back of the journal, I noticed it was a few minutes before 10 a.m.

After I finished packing my gear, I used the toilet, concentrating on making sure my system was adequately emptied to avoid a pit stop for at least a few hours.

At 10:25 a.m., I said a silent prayer for safe travel and that my home would not be molested while on my travels. I slung my duffel bag over my right shoulder and left my apartment, carefully locking the deadbolt, as well as the lock in the doorknob. I started to walk down the hallway.

Wait! Did I check to make sure the door was locked? My undiagnosed obsessive-compulsive behavior was kicking in. I walked back to check the door, grabbing the doorknob and twisting it again. *Better safe than sorry,* I thought. Lord knows I didn't want to fixate on a possibly unlocked door the entire trip. No worries! The door was, in fact, locked tight. Secured!

I had often wondered if I had some degree of Obsessive Compulsive Disorder. The trouble was that I could never refer to it as "OCD." The letters were in the *wrong* alphabetical order. Now, "CDO" made more sense to me.

I had retraced my steps as I again walked through the hallway to the front entrance of the apartment building, to the parking lot where I hoped to find Bob and a rental truck, our chariot to an exciting adventure.

Chapter Six

Musical Mayhem: The Search for Audio Bliss

The sky was clear and the sun shone down on Bob proudly standing next to the big yellow 14-foot Ryder rental truck, which had been jam-packed with his art the previous day.

As I approached Bob, I studied his fashion makeover. Atop his head was a well-worn vintage tractor baseball cap, circa 1980s, with the bold yellow leaping stag logo stitched above an uppercase JOHN DEERE.

Nice, I thought, *an earthy, all-American choice.*

The bill of his cap barely touched his classic Sixties thick, black-rimmed glasses, nothing fancy. On his torso, he wore a black design-free sweatshirt that wouldn't arouse the same attention as if it had a sports team or provocative music group logo. He was wearing comfortably-fitting Levi denim blue jeans.

Another good choice! Not a fancy designer brand with flashy stitching to attract unwanted scrutiny.

His footwear: White canvas Converse All-Star Chuck Taylors.

Classic!

His fashion ensemble for the road trip was near perfect. Except for the diamond-stud earring in his earlobe and the dozen bracelets on his right arm, I would have thought he was a farmer from Iowa. As he arrived, he could best be identified as a farmer from Chicago's gay epicenter, Boys Town.

"The hat is a nice touch. Well done!" I complimented my roadside fashion plate as he placed his hands on his hips, striking a stylish pose. "It goes well with your earring and all those bracelets."

"Small steps, my friend. Small steps," Bob said with a hint of a smile. "Ten minutes at a Salvation Army outlet and I'm a new man. Boring, but new." He started to step toward his side of the truck. "I'll drive."

"Sounds good to me." I opened the truck door, threw my one bag into the passenger's side, and climbed in. The cab was bigger than I had expected; plenty of room for my six-foot-tall frame with long legs to fit beyond my duffel bag.

Bob took his place in the driver's seat, buckled up, and turned the key to start the engine. In the cup-holders, I spied two large-sized Dunkin Donuts coffee cups and smiled broadly. Bob noticed. He was proud.

"I got us coffee," he said. "Ain't I a thoughtful guy? I didn't know how you took it, so there's cream and sugar in the bag."

"Thanks, dude," I said as I dug through the bag for one cream and two sugars. "Take 53 south and follow the signs to Joliet. We pick up 80 west near there." I pulled out my road atlas with the path clearly highlighted with a bright yellow marker.

"Please don't call me dude! Ever!"

Nice start for a week in a small truck, I thought.

"Sorry. Duly noted," I said, a bit surprised by his outburst, and then I returned to my map.

"Do you have star charts, too?" he said with more than a hint of sarcasm.

"Ha, ha," I said dryly. "Just trying to be organized." I took the plastic cover off the coffee cup and started to mix in the appropriate proportions of cream and sugar. Like a science experiment, I was careful to add just enough milk to achieve the proper shade of caramel brown for my taste: not too dark and not too light; perfection in a paper cup.

As he revved up the engine and put the truck in gear, the vehicle jerked forward and my coffee splashed about, soaking my hand. I grabbed napkins from the paper bag to mop up the mess.

"Give me a second," I pleaded, not wanting to waste a single drop of my go-go juice. Quickly I secured the coffee cup lid and put on my shoulder-harness seat belt. With the distinctive click, I was ready.

"Reset the trip odometer, please. Then we can track our progress," I said, concerned about accurately recording our daily mileage.

Bob pressed the button clearing the trip odometer so it read zero. I checked my wristwatch: 10:30 a.m. on the dot.

As I rolled down the window, I looked at Bob with a big smile and said, "Let's do it!"

We pulled out of my apartment complex and onto the road. I was practically giddy with excitement. We were heading on an adventure, an adventure to the great, Wild West. Pulling onto the highway, I thought about the countless times I drove on Route 53 south and fantasized about driving to the West Coast, to California. Today, my dream was a reality.

"This is so exciting! Adventure around every corner," I beamed.

"No, there's a McDonald's around every corner," Bob corrected, making sure my balloon stayed grounded. He teased, "But I think your enthusiasm is really cute, Michael."

"Fuck you," was my retort, given with a big toothy grin. It was an uncreative, lame response, but it served its purpose of letting him know I didn't appreciate the early-morning rib.

The sky was a brilliant blue, with the sun shining. There was light traffic, a warm breeze and the open road. I sipped my tepid coffee, took a deep breath, and looked down at my map. All of the pieces were coming together as we embarked on our epic excursion to California. Then it occurred to me that all of my senses were in a state of bliss, but one. Something was missing from the perfect road trip equation: Music!

I pulled out my ultimate travel mix-tape from my bag and went to slip it into the cassette player, but I couldn't find the slot.

"Where do I play my tape?" I asked Bob, certain there was some hi-tech, well-designed opening I didn't see, maybe some kind of hidden switch.

"I didn't ask for a truck with a cassette player. I figured a radio would do," Bob said matter-of-factly, unaware of the impact this decision would have on me. "I didn't think it was a big deal. You're okay with that, right?"

Panic! Having completed a couple of cross-country road trips before, I knew all too well the shortfalls of relying on radio. Chicago had several cool radio stations, my favorite being WXRT where the musical mix included great songs from the past, present along with new, alternative bands on the verge of stardom. On the road though, except for airwaves near Los Angeles, we'd be restricted to Radio Purgatory where Talk Radio, Oldies and Top 40 stations reigned supreme, employing lame deejays hosting *morning zoos*, trying desperately to be wacky. Worst still were the homegrown, poorly produced local ads that were rarely so bad, they'd be good. Nope, my experience was sucky radio ads so bad they were unbearable to listen to on the airwaves. Long nails on a chalk-dry blackboard would be a blissful sound in comparison.

"Sure. Fine," I said under my breath, as if I had just been offered an ice water enema. "No problem."

I felt like Bruce Willis's Butch Coolidge character in *Pulp Fiction* trying to explain to his French girlfriend Fabienne that it was his fault that he didn't explain to her the extreme importance of his father's wristwatch – the one kept hidden up his dad's ass for several years while in a Hanoi POW camp – the one she had accidently left behind in his apartment prior to their need to skip town.

Bob turned on the radio to the closing saccharine-drenched strains of Barry Manilow's "I Write the Songs," as it bled into "Come Sail Away" by Styx. Had a Michael Bolton song come next, it would have been the Trilogy of Terror of the most unholy of relatively contemporary pop songs. It was a sign. Bad voodoo left behind from the previous drivers who obviously had no sense of musical taste, tuning into a very lame station. Not the way one wants to start an adventure, *a quest*. Odysseus had the Cyclops, six-headed Scylla and the Sirens to contend with on his journey. We had Manilow, Styx and Bolton! Quickly I turned the knob and tuned in 93.1 on the FM dial, WXRT, the musical mecca of cool Chicago radio. As the signal locked in, the bass line from "Jamming" by Bob Marley and The Wailers greeted us. *Thank goodness and crank it up!* I thought. Marley was the best musical antidote to the pop poison we had just ingested. As long as the signal held, we had righteous music. I dreaded the signal fading, just as the early explorers feared falling off the edge of the earth.

Did I lock my apartment door?

Chapter Seven

The First Time I Met Bob

Naked Tap-Dancing Zebra Women. Prior to meeting Bob, I had never witnessed a performance by Naked Tap-Dancing Zebra Women. At first glance, one might think this was the name of some 1980s New Wave rock band. But it wasn't. It was a group of three completely nude (except for a tiny, black G-string) women with their bodies painted, by Bob, to look like zebras ...and they tap-danced!

Ask fifty people to define what is *art,* and you'll get fifty different answers. Even the art world itself has had trouble with a definitive answer. Marcel Duchamp challenged the classic, traditional idea of art in 1917, when he took a common urinal and placed it in an exhibition calling it, *Fountain.* About forty-five years later, Andy Warhol painted a Campbell's soup can label and made it as famous as the Mona Lisa. And now, in the rich tradition of challenging the very definition of art, Robert A. Fischer (formal twin to "Bob") produced: *Naked Tap-Dancing Zebra Women.*

This was just one of the acts showcased at *Robert A. Fischer's Cirkus of the Bizzarte*, a neo-vaudevillian, performance art extravaganza held at the Germania Club. The Victorian-era structure, built in 1889 on one of the shortest streets in Chicago near the corner of North Avenue and Clark Street, stood in the shadows of Sandburg Village. The event was held on a Saturday night, October 30, 1982, appropriately Halloween eve, and for a mere $15 admission price, patrons could experience Bob's dark and twisted vision of a modern day urban freak show. Little did I know that attending this event would forever change my life.

The Cirkus of the Bizzarte was not the family-friendly Barnum & Bailey-type of events I had attended as a boy. It was an underground celebration of decadence and debauchery inspired by the Magic Theater featured in Herman Hesse's novel, *Steppenwolf*. Fischer's event had a carnival setting created to seduce one's senses: visual stimuli; haunting music; erotic scents; intoxicating drinks; and sensuous caresses as you slipped through the throngs of attendees. Instead of elephants, clowns or laughing children, patrons of the *Cirkus* witnessed fire-eaters, jugglers, strippers, exhibitionists, voyeurs and of course, plenty of performance artists such as the Naked Tap-Dancing Zebra Women and Mistress Regina, the Leather Goddess, who performed in the Whips and Lips *Cirkus of Fetishes*. Also featured on the promotional handbill designed to look like an old circus poster was a popular '80s Chicago area rock band named Jinx, and the "tickler of the ivories and master of the mighty organ," Hal Pearl, a pianist/organist who had accompanied silent films in movie theaters, as well as provided music for Aragon Ballroom dances during the Big Band era. Of course, my friend Bob had been the Ring Master for this ultra-kinky three-ring spectacle.

Bob staged these events to showcase his paintings, or *Bizzarte,* as he named them. They consisted of colorful portraits of celebrities, socialites and social outcasts, many of which had costume jewelry fastened to the canvas in appropriate areas around necks or earlobes, giving the image a

3-D feel. Like Warhol, his canvas paintings were bright, kaleidoscopic, pop interpretations of the famous, the erotic, and the grotesque.

"It's my job as an artist not to paint pretty pictures, but to confront people, to challenge and change their points of view," Bob once told me. The London Times Art critic John Russell Taylor referred to Bob as "the centre of outrage in America." Now, this purveyor of outrage was producing a multi-dimensional exhibition of the offbeat, exotic, and erotic in Chicago.

The stage at the Germania Club provided the space for the show, while the walls of the club acted as a gallery for Bob's artwork. The event itself though, was also a work of art with the performers as his palette of paint, so to speak, and the event as his canvas. These events were never publicly advertised in newspapers, radio or TV with conventional ads. Instead, Bob published eight to twelve page newspapers with snappy text, intriguing promises of exotic, offbeat talent, and images of Bob and his creative team from prior events.

I had just started dating a woman who worked at an advertising agency. She had secured tickets for *Cirkus*, and wanting to surprise me, simply told me to dress for a *provocative* Halloween party. I didn't own anything provocative and it was a very last-minute request, so I needed to create something quickly. Using a simple black mask and some face paint, I developed *Satan The Clown*, a kind of scary, demented circus freak whose smile brought more terror than laughter. I wore a pair of fingerless, leather gloves to give my alter-persona a subtle sinister touch.

My date accompanied me in her skimpy, sexy black and white silk French maid's outfit, complete with naughty thigh-high nylons, stiletto heals, and a black mask over her eyes to conceal her identity. We were sexy, yet creepy. We fit right in.

The day after the event, I wrote a letter to the event's creator, Robert A. Fischer. I explained that I had attended the *Cirkus of the Bizzarte* and that it was "the most decadent and disgusting display of humanity that I've ever seen." I went on to explain that I loved every minute of it, and asked how I could get involved in future productions.

Bob called me and we set a time to meet for dinner near his apartment on Wells Street, just south of North Avenue in Old Town. We met at a neighborhood restaurant, nothing fancy, and after about an hour of conversation about our common passion for music, art and producing cultural events, Bob offered me the job of being his production manager for his next event, a prom for adults. At that time, my job producing cultural events at a college involved promoting programs that included: stand-up comedians Jay Leno, Jerry Seinfeld, and Richard Lewis; musical talent Wynton and Branford Marsalis, Muddy Waters, Psychedelic Furs, and Joan Jett; and a wide variety of novelty acts who juggled chainsaws, performed with ventriloquist dummies, and hypnotized students. The opportunity to leap from mainstream talent to something more exotic, like working with Naked Tap-Dancing Zebra Women, was an exciting new territory for me to explore. So, it took only a moment for me to shake Bob's hand as I agreed to be his partner in creating neo-vaudevillian, performance art extravaganzas for the next few years.

During my unconventional cultural apprenticeship with him, we soon became fast friends and confidants, often sharing our innermost secrets and fears…or so I thought.

Chapter Eight

Traveling 55 mph in an 80 mph World

"How far have we gone?" I asked Bob, motioning towards the trip odometer.

"About thirty-five miles," Bob noted.

"Only one-thousand nine-hundred and forty more miles to go," I quickly calculated. I couldn't mask my mild disappointment as I added, " I thought we were further along."

We had barely started our journey, yet I craved more substantial progress. We needed to make up some time and increase our speed. Our vehicle was now on Route 355, going south, approaching Joliet and our eventual rendezvous with Route 80, which would be our gateway to the West. As we drove along the highway, I patiently waited for Bob to challenge the truck's engine and cruise at a faster pace. At 55 miles per hour, it took about two hours to achieve a little more than one hundred miles of progress, depending on traffic, but at 70 miles per hour, we'd make much better time.

As we cruised down the road, I realized that there was very little traffic, and the telephone poles and road signs were passing at a rather sluggish rate.

"C'mon, step on it, Bob. Don't be such a wimp, we're barely going the speed limit," I playfully needled the man behind the wheel.

Bob smiled and gave me a devilish look, "You got it!"

His right white canvas gym shoe pressed down hard on the gas pedal, but the engine did not react. He repeated the action, this time pressing down so hard that he almost stood up in his seat. Nothing. No power boost. No increase in speed. Bob looked bewildered and somewhat puzzled as he turned to me with a comically grimaced face.

Perhaps at face value Bob and I looked like we had nothing in common, but one thing we did share was a total *lack of patience*. This trait didn't come in handy with our next discovery about our truck.

"What the fuck!" I'm not a mechanical genius, but I was able to reason that the shop must have added some kind of governor to regulate the gas going to the carburetor. This device would maintain a near-constant speed regardless of how much we stepped on the gas pedal. The result was a maximum vehicle speed of 55 miles per hour, period. Not 56 mph or even 57 mph, but only 55 mph. Achieving *double nickels* on most roads would not be an issue, but on the open highways we would be on now, the speed limit was set at 65 mph, which meant 70 to 75 mph with relaxed enforcement by the state police. We were now limited to driving a full ten to 20 miles per hour slower than our colleagues on the road. What we would save on gas, would certainly take its toll on our stress levels. So, to sum up our situation at this junction: We didn't have decent music and didn't have real speed. The only joy we had was rolling down the windows and making an *airplane wing* with an outside arm, secretly wishing the effort would reduce wind sheer and propel our vehicle a few miles per hour faster.

Everyone passed us by as we struggled to commute at 55 mph in the 65 mph zone.

"THIS REALLY SUCKS!" we both screamed in unison as our cruel reality began to sink in.

A large white Winnebago, a whale of a recreational vehicle normally confined to the slowest lane, passed us with ease. The female driver had a crimson, stacked hairstyle that would challenge Marge Simpson's phallic blue tresses for sheer height.

"The higher the hair, the closer to God," I said with a slight drawl.

As she drove by, she defiantly shook her fist at us, her face spasmed with shock as if she had just been administered an ice-water enema. I could only surmise that she was repulsed by our lethargic pace, cursing the apparent hamsters harnessed underneath our hood.

Another mobile mansion flew by us moments later and the old guy behind the wheel flipped us off. The white-haired woman in the passenger seat wearing a pink baseball cap, was screaming at us through a closed window. I could clearly read her lips yelling, "Go faster, asshole!"

Ironically as they passed us, we noted the "What would Jesus do?" sticker on their bumper.

"I love Christians, " Bob dryly commented.

"A-men," I said quietly under my breath. "Y'know, I *really* hate this," I declared more loudly. "It's like life is passing us by."

"You should be used to it," he teased.

The joy of the open road quickly dissipated.

"Well let's be Zen about this," Bob said philosophically. "We have no option but to learn patience."

He was right. Slow down, breathe, and embrace our snail-paced travel.

Chapter Nine

A Rolling Confessional on
The Road to Self-Discovery

Since Bob was driving, it was my responsibility to act as navigator and determine our route of travel.

"What's our travel goal today?"

Bob thought for a moment, "I was hoping for Lincoln, Nebraska, but now I'm thinking Omaha."

"Doable," I said as I studied the road atlas and guessed it would be a reasonable distance to achieve our first day out. We were currently driving through Peoria via Route 55, a number that mocked our current fate in truck speedometer readings. Within a few minutes we would reach Route 80 which would take us directly west to Iowa and eventually Nebraska.

There's nothing like an open road and lots of flat, boring scenery to make one's mind wander. I began to think about my recent romantic disaster and wondered what would be next for me. Four months earlier in January, I had left a long relationship. Jennifer and I had been together about six years, lived together for half that, and recently had moved apart. As

1997 began, I decided it was time to end things and move on; start the new year fresh with a clean slate.

Unfortunately, my mind had made a decision for the future while my heart was still quite involved in the past. Each day was a struggle to not call her, work to resolve our problems and resume our relationship. That's why this road trip had sounded so appealing. It would provide me an opportunity to think about things, assess what I had, consider what I wanted, and then strategize my next steps.

To understand Bob Fischer and his art, one must examine his background and make no assumptions. For instance, his college degree wasn't in art, but psychology.

"I went to college to avoid the draft," Bob once proudly admitted to me, "I certainly would have died in basic training." An accurate assessment for an over-weight, self-described freak who was often chosen last for every team in gym class.

It made sense for Bob to embrace his brains over brawn and choose Psychology as a major at Roosevelt University in Chicago to better understand people and the way they behave, based on their environment. He once told me that he never expected to become a *shrink*, but it was obvious that his education in psychology influenced his art, as well as bolstered his innate ability to better understand and communicate with the stable of models, performers, production people and friends he worked with daily. I guess I fit into at least two of those categories. I was both a friend and his production manager for most of his events in the 1980s.

One other important thing to know about Bob was that he rarely filtered his comments as he spoke with you. He told you what he felt you needed to know, not necessarily what you wanted to hear. For our relationship, this trait had been the catalyst for several arguments and fights, as his sometimes-critical remarks or unsolicited advice came off as arrogant and hurtful. Although the end result may have been unintentional, Bob's blunt honesty and glib delivery often made it difficult for me to interpret if he was being facetious or sincere.

To best understand me, I need to provide full disclosure: I was a true extrovert and often needed to process my thoughts and feelings out loud. As I sought solutions to my problems, I relied on *thoroughly* talking about a topic with a friend, and through this process, I developed answers to my questions.

While on the road, Bob and I were immured in our truck cab, like a rolling, portable Roman Catholic confessional. Now, Bob was about to become my confessor and therapist on a lengthy road trip analysis session.

"Bless me father, for I have sinned," I said softly as we cruised down the road.

"What?" Bob offered, not hearing a word, just knowing I said something.

"Nothing," I smiled. "I was just wondering if you'd be open to helping me sort through something."

Bob thought for a moment. "Sure. We got nothing else to do."

I paused for a few seconds, collecting my thoughts and determining the best way to begin. After several months of an emotional odyssey, I wanted to distill the facts efficiently so not to go down any unnecessary paths.

"I don't know if I made the right decision," I said slowly, carefully selecting my words.

"Huh?"

"Leaving Jennifer. Getting out of the relationship. I don't know if leaving her was the right decision. "

Bob didn't respond for a while and just stared out at the road. I think he was pulling together the few bits and pieces about the relationship I had shared with him over time.

"Okay. Let's review," he began, like a prosecuting attorney during a closing argument. "She asks for time apart from you. You move out."

"Right."

"Then, you two kind of date for a couple of months. Go out on weekends."

"Right."

"You say it's over earlier this year, in January, I believe. And now, it's been four months with no contact, right?"

Yes, that's right." His timeline and facts were accurate.

Bob thought for a moment, looking like an accountant adding up a few figures in his mind.

"Sounds over to me," he said with a shrug.

"Not if we are taking *a break*," I argued. Somehow, in my mind, I had convinced myself that maybe the break up was not so final. It could be just a temporary situation, a time for reflection and assessment.

"Was that agreed upon?" Bob asked, back in lawyer mode.

"Not exactly. It was kind of inferred. I assumed the door remained open to return."

Bob laughed. In fact, he laughed so hard it was contagious and I joined him in the joke. Then, it occurred to me, he wasn't laughing with me, he was laughing *at* me. I gently protested.

"What? I'm being optimistic."

"More like delusional," he said smiling.

"Really?" My question was heartfelt and I started to feel pretty clueless about the situation.

"You two were together a long time."

"Six years," I nodded. "We had our moments."

"Moments? What the fuck is a moment?"

"Yeah, I guess you're right," I said reluctantly and crestfallen. Somehow six years didn't seem that long to me. It felt like we had just met and been dating a short time. That was enough for me, and she didn't seem to want more, at least she never spoke about it.

"Why do you think you stayed with her so long?"

Fair question, I thought to myself. I started to pull together a quick laundry list of reasons.

"She was good for me." I began counting off my list, "She convinced me to get my Masters degree. Motivated me to do my photography and gallery shows. She was a great editor for my writing…"

"Sounds like delusion," he said, cutting me off before I continued. "She sounds more like a business partner than a romantic partner to me. And, more important, it sounds like a co-dependency."

"Co-dependency?"

He began to pull from his background in psychology, "As I understand it, co-dependency occurs when you assess your self-worth through another person and seek their approval."

I nodded slowly, allowing time to process what he had just said. His remark made a lot of sense to me.

"There's a lot going on here," he continued. "You define the relationship in *your* terms. I don't get a sense that you are willing to meet her half way on things. You don't even vacation together, right?"

He was right. I did rely on her feedback and approval. He was also right about our vacations. Even though we had gone on trips together earlier in our relationship, we were now vacationing separately. The year before, she had wanted to go to India and I wanted to go to Thailand. We couldn't compromise so we took separate vacations.

"True. We couldn't find a place we both wanted to visit."

I checked my mental list for another reason why we had remained together.

"We were good lovers," I declared, hoping to secure at least one solid reason to justify our lengthy, yet fruitless relationship. "The sex was good."

"Fucking doesn't equal love!" Bob looked directly at me, pulling his eyes off the road for a moment, "We've had this discussion before. You mistake lust for love. The question is: do you really want to spend the rest of your life with her?"

Good question, I thought. Unfortunately, I didn't have a definitive answer. And that truly was the real problem between Jennifer and me. I had long suffered from *Analysis Paralysis*, as decisions never came easy to me. When it came to our relationship, I had labored over this question practically every day for the entire time Jennifer and I were together. Of course, we first met with a sexy fling at a conference. I had mistaken lust for love and playfully daydreamed of a future together. That assessment changed though, as time progressed and reality set in. I kept her at a slight emotional distance. I tended to over-think even the simplest of decisions, always seeking back-up plans and additional choices, just in case. After my experience with my wife, Candy – leaving me to my utter surprise for a woman – I was overly-cautious about committing my heart so fully to another person. I didn't want to go through all of that emotional turmoil and torture again.

It made sense to keep our relationship in neutral. Little did I know how exhausting it would be to keep spinning my wheels without making any progress. Every few months, I'd have a panic attack, thinking about our relationship and committing to marriage. The only thing that helped me retain my calm was the idea of taking life one day at a time and not pushing for more. Jennifer seemed okay with that and we rarely spoke of marriage and settling down, unless someone in her circle of friends did so. Even then, it was a discussion for a few days that would eventually pass, and then we returned to the status quo. At which point, I could breathe again.

I was exhausted just rethinking it all again in the truck. *Shit! Do I really want this for the rest of my life?*

Bob looked really impatient with my lack of a response. This discussion was becoming very stressful for me. I struggled for an answer to Bob's question, but I didn't have one readily available.

"Not sure," I said quietly.

He challenged me, `"Yes, you are!"

"Things were okay until her friends told her to give me an ultimatum."

"Shit or get off the pot."

"Something like that."

"Were you happy?"

That was another fair question in need of an answer. Bob was a very good therapist. I took a few moments to think about it.

Besides my fear of commitment, I was a man-child with little desire to grow up and mature. Like many of my male friends, I embraced the Peter Pan Syndrome like it was a fun-filled amusement park ride and I had a pocketful of tickets. I was the epitome of the pleasure-seeking id, with an insatiable desire for instant gratification and little concern for being a responsible partner. I worked hard at my job, but played hard as well. "I'll sleep when I die" was my motto as I crammed more entertainment-related activities into a week than others did in a month. It wasn't uncommon for me to go to a new film release in the afternoon, grab dinner, check out the *hot ticket* concert for the evening, and then hit a night club or two to dance until dawn before coming home.

My close male friends shared the same attitude.

Why settle down and marry, unless you want children? Having children was not important to me just yet, so I was in no hurry. Jennifer wasn't eager for kids either, so I thought we were on the same page. We loved to play together. We had good times. We laughed. *But did we laugh most days?* As I gave it serious thought, I answered honestly.

"We were happy maybe two days out of five."

"Really? Listen to yourself." Bob took a breath and looked me in the eye. "Don't you deserve more?" He paused. "At least three days out of five?" His eyes returned to the road and I looked down, allowing time to absorb his observation.

It was simple, yet significant. For me, it was a moment of clarity.

"I guess you're right," I admitted sheepishly.

"If your relationship had felt right, you'd have asked her to marry you. Your hesitation seems to me that you feel you're *settling* by choosing her."

"Marriage is a big commitment," I said, defending my hesitation. "I don't want to make another mistake."

"You didn't make a mistake with your first wife. She wasn't being honest with you. And Jennifer is not Candy."

"Just because Candy fucked you over doesn't mean Jennifer would," Bob said, his voice showing some frustration. I wasn't connecting the dots as fast as he had as an outside observer. I had been too close to it all.

"And you told me that she didn't believe in you," he continued making his point. "She didn't believe your book would get published. And more importantly, she didn't love you unconditionally or accept you for who you were."

I had published a book as part of my Masters degree work on diversity. It was the first in the field to address diversity concerns at a community college and a small academic press published it. Even after I had received a printed copy of the book in the mail, she was hesitant to believe that I had actually accomplished that goal. Even as she held a copy of the book in her hand, she wouldn't pat me on the back and say, "good job!"

However, Bob wasn't entirely correct. It was I who didn't love her unconditionally or accept her for who she was. I wasn't a very good partner. Each year, when it was time to renew the lease for our apartment, I also insisted we assess our relationship and decide if we wanted to continue. I thought it was a reasonable thing to do, but it's tough for either party to make a relationship truly work, especially if there's an annual evaluation that allows for the two to part. I hadn't been fair to her and I felt guilty.

"I just don't know." I shook my head sadly, confused by all of the emotional data running through my mind.

Bob sighed loudly. I could sense his growing frustration with me.

"You know what your problem is? *You don't want to take responsibility for your own life,*" he said. If he had been filtering his comments and trying to be gentle before, he was now going to be direct, honest, and blunt.

"It's like your life at Harper College. You want to be a writer, yet you stay there. It's safe. You have a steady paycheck. Well, I think you're afraid to take risks! You want the success without the sweat. You want to be rescued! You want me to tell you that you've made the right decision! Well, I can't do that. That's not *my responsibility.* You need to take responsibility to make things happen in your own life!"

His assessment of me may have been accurate, but his delivery seemed hurtful and sanctimonious. I felt attacked.

I didn't appreciate *him* telling me what was wrong with my life, even if I had asked. His life wasn't perfect. The way I saw it, he didn't take risks either. His wife Paula had worked to pay many of the bills early in his career, allowing him to be an artist. Oh sure, he contributed, but she was his safety net. I didn't have a Paula in my life.

Besides, what did *he* know? Bob had experienced some success, however it wasn't like he was a well-respected member of the art world having his work showcased in museums. His paintings were featured in small galleries and in *Penthouse* magazine. As far as I could see, much of his success happened by pairing off with the right people. Paula opened him up to painting and helped pay the bills, and Edward was affluent. Bob had his rich sugar daddy and now he was being mean to me.

Sure I had asked for his opinion, yet somehow I expected it would have mirrored mine. I felt cornered, wounded, and I lashed out at him.

"Fuck you!" Not a great retort, however it was an efficient release for my pent-up anger.

"What's wrong? It's the truth!"

"Yeah, right! Who are you to give me advice about my life and relationships? It's not like you are a glowing example of the Good Partner. You just dumped Paula for Edward after three children and a 20-year marriage."

"It's complicated." Bob's response was barely audible.

Now it was my turn to deliver the ugly truth as I barked out, "No, it's pretty fucked up for Paula is what it is!"

The mood had gotten ugly and the truck cab was building up steam like a pressure cooker on a full flame. Something had to give, and I had had enough of this conversation for now.

After a deep breath and ten count, I decided it was best to play peacemaker and diffuse the situation. I had plenty of respect for his talent and ability as an artist, but I resented the fact that he didn't have to survive on his own output. He didn't have rent and monthly utilities hanging over his head as I did.

To be fair, artists historically often had sponsors, financial angels, to underwrite their projects. I guessed Bob was following this tradition. Besides I didn't mean to lash out at him as he was only trying to help. He cared enough about me to be honest. The truth stung though, and I needed to take a step back and think about his observations.

"Hey, I didn't mean to get so angry," I apologized. "It's the heat and I'm hungry. What do you say we stop and take a breather?"

I could see an upcoming exit sign off in the distance with a myriad of fast food logos. I glanced at my watch and it was nearly 2:30 p.m., long past lunchtime.

"It's fine," he grumbled.

This wasn't the first time that we had raised our voices in our lengthy history together. Like brothers, we tended to press each other's emotional hot buttons, yell, clear the air, and then move on as if it hadn't happened. Someone had once said to me that the best friends are those with the shortest memories, and when it came to fights between us, we were quick to forget the cause of the crisis, and then move on to another conversation.

"So, what's your pleasure?" I squinted to read the fast food options coming up at the next exit. "Mickey D's, Wendy's or Taco Bell?"

"I think we deserve a break today."

"McDonald's it is!" Quarter Pounders with cheese were a guilty pleasure of mine, so the decision wasn't hard to agree with. "It's funny. Whenever I travel out of the country, the first stop I make when I come home is McDonald's for a Quarter Pounder."

"Because it's so All-American and wholesome?"

"No, I just love the taste. I actually crave them as soon as I get off a plane."

I thought for a moment. "You know, I don't understand where I get my wanderlust. I've been to several world capitals:

London, Paris, Rome, Cairo. Yet, as a kid, my family barely ventured beyond our state border. In fact, our Big Family Vacation most summers was to northern Wisconsin and the Dells."

"Ah, the Wisconsin Dells, the Coney Island of the Midwest," Bob said with a chuckle.

I added, "Yep, the exotic Fort Dells and the nearby Paul Bunyan Restaurant, complete with huge statues of Paul, with Babe, his Blue Ox, and a fake lumberjack setting. Talk about a low-budget Disneyland."

We pulled off the highway and onto the exit ramp, turned right after a quarter of a mile, and headed for the big Golden Arches.

"You know, I remember a time when every exit wasn't so generic," I reminisced. "There were actual ma and pa restaurants that weren't part of a chain and you could experience local flavor."

"We're an hour or so outside Des Moines. I'm not sure how exotic our choices would have been," Bob countered.

I studied all of the messy specks on our windshield and observed, "Hey, we have quite a bug cemetery developing on the window. When we get gas, I'll have to scrape off the carcasses."

It would be important for me to have an unobstructed view as we continued our journey.

Chapter Ten

Sex Tales

"This is probably a good time to inform you that I don't have a driver's license," I said to Bob as we walked back to the truck after having lunch.

Before he could react, I continued with a fast and furious manic delivery, "I'm prone to hallucinations. Flashbacks from 'Nam, you see: big palm trees dancing across the road; evil robot gladiators tailgating our vehicle in fuel-injected chariots; stripper nuns in mortal combat with dominatrix gnomes! Wait! Maybe that last one wasn't exactly a hallucination. Hmm! Weird shit! As it stands, my doctor forbids me to drive. Unless it's a Formula One car, and then all bets are off!"

Bob chuckled at my Hunter-Thompson-on-drugs-like rant, "Okay, nice. Now, drive!"

It felt good to share a lighter moment with Bob. What's the point of a road trip if you aren't getting any kicks? Besides, we needed to cleanse our palettes from our intense and upsetting discussion prior to our lunch stop.

I began my shift behind the wheel by heading to a nearby gas station to fill up our tank, clean the windows, and grab a few snacks and ice cold beverages for the road. We hopped back on I-80 and headed west.

Once again, the boredom of the flat, open road got my mind to wander and I started to process not only what Bob and I had talked about earlier, but other related concerns as well. One issue was particularly awkward to discuss. It had bothered me for quite awhile and I suppose there was no time like the present to bring it up.

About six months earlier, Bob's most recent paintings were on display at a gallery in Chicago and his new beau Edward, after having a few cocktails, had unceremoniously *outed* Bob to his friends at the event. Edward had told my girlfriend Jennifer that he and Bob were lovers and we were invited to come visit them *anytime* in Palm Springs. When Jennifer shared this with me, it really took me by surprise. I had been friends with Bob for almost 15 years and knew his wife Paula and his three kids very well.

Never in all that time did I think that Bob might be or could be gay. If anything, he was a colorful eccentric artist, in a Salvador Dali kind of way. Little did I know he was eccentric in more of a Liberace kind of way. After all that time, how did I *not* know he was gay? It was time to discuss the Big Gay Elephant in the truck cab.

"So, you and I really haven't had a chance to talk about you." I swallowed hard and took a deep breath. Bob and I could always talk about anything. Now, I needed to get the answer to a very pressing question. "Bob, you were married to Paula for almost 20 years and had three kids. When did you realize you were gay?"

Without hesitation and with a lot of enthusiasm, Bob delivered a response that, as always, was frank, direct and uncensored, "I always knew I loved cock!"

No beating around the bush for Bob. I nodded and smiled with friendly support.

"When I used to live on Wells Street," he offered. "I'd go off for anonymous sex in the back of the Bijou Theater, then go back to my wife. Since it was anonymous, it wasn't cheating to me."

The Bijou Theater has screened gay adult films in Old Town since 1970, a time when The Second City, The Earl of Old Town, and Piper's Alley were a magnet for members of the counterculture, and the epicenter for hippies in Chicago. In fact not far from the Bijou was a primo head shop called Bizarre Bazaar, where a person could score bongs, pipes, pipe screens and papers, as well as tie-dyed clothing, black light posters, underground comics and incense. Nirvana for many of my high school buddies!

I needed a little clarification, "So, you got-it-on in a movie theater?"

I was wondering how one could discreetly hump someone in what I assumed were rigid old movie theater seats, which were often small with firm, unmovable arm rests.

"Got it on? What is this 1973?" Bob snickered and then responded, "Hand jobs. Maybe the occasional blow job."

"Ah," I again nodded, that made more sense to me. "So you were more or less bi- while you were married?"

"No, I was always gay and just fucked my wife to keep my cover."

"So let's fast forward to your move to L.A.," I sat up in my seat and checked my two rearview mirrors. "How did you meet Edward?"

"When I was living in North Hollywood, I went to a gay married men's group and had a wonderful group leader who encouraged me to start my own group in Palm Springs. I wanted to learn about the 'coming out' process, so I ran an ad in a local gay rag. Something like," Bob paused for a moment to recall the ad. He looked up into space and used his right hand to place the words in an imaginary ad in front of the windshield. "Married, gay, coming out, don't deal with these issues alone. Gay married men's group now forming. Call Bob. Use discretion. And then, my phone number."

Bob sipped some of his icy cold beverage from our last stop. Then, he continued, "I got some calls, but mostly from married men wanting to blow me. So, I'm ready to give up, but Edward calls late one night. He says he could be helpful to the group because he came out shortly after his divorce. He wanted to meet, but I was worried about getting caught by Paula, so I refused. But Ed was persistent. He called again and again. So, one night, when the kids were asleep and Paula was off playing Bingo, or something, I agreed to meet him at his house."

"Really?" I interrupted. "Weren't you taking a big risk?" Not only could Bob get caught by Paula, he was meeting a stranger on his own turf.

Bob continued, "Well, he said he had a 'big house with an electric gate,' so I felt somewhat safe. Which in retrospect is absurd. Like a killer couldn't have money, or something.

"As I drove over though, in the back of my mind, I was worried that he could be a serial killer: A Palm Springs Jeffrey Dahmer or something. So, I decided that I wouldn't eat or drink anything unless he did, too! It made sense to me to be extra careful."

"Good thought!" I interjected. "I did the same in Thailand when I went to a sex show last year."

"Sex show?" Bob's eyes widened. I couldn't tell if he was intrigued or impressed with my admission. I was his clean, Catholic, Polish friend, and I had just revealed potentially corrupt behavior.

"Yeah, I was always curious about what I'd see," I said sheepishly. "I'm so Catholic though! It's funny. My first attempt to see a sex show was actually in London, in Soho back in 1986. I think it was actually called a 'Bed Show' at this place."

I took a moment to recall the sordid details and continued, "It was late at night and I was investigating the backstreets of Soho. I saw this big neon sign that said 'Bed Show' in a storefront window with a small box office nearby, next to this beaded curtain you have to walk through to enter. Some guy, a barker, was out front persuading guys to come on in to their private booths."

I went on to tell Bob how I watched from across the street for about ten minutes, however I didn't cross the street. I was really paranoid that someone I knew would see me go in the place. Which was *really stupid* because I didn't know anyone in London at the time, and it was late at night and dark. So, I walked around the block a couple of times, mustered up some courage, and walked to the box office. I paid some kind of cover charge and then was led into this small booth.

"There was a small wooden stool," I continued. "So I sat down and there was a window in front of me, but there was something blocking the view. Just below the window, I noticed a metal box that you had to put a British pound coin in and then turn the knob, just like putting a penny into an old gumball machine. I discovered that once you did, the blind opened, and for a few minutes you viewed this nude woman playing with herself. So, I deposited a coin, turned the crank, and watched this attractive young blonde going through the motions of caressing herself, but it wasn't very passionate or convincing.

"Not arousing at all," I told Bob. "In fact, for me it was depressing. I'm thinking, 'how sad!' This woman has to do this to make a living, maybe to feed a kid or something."

"Oh my gawd, you are so-o-o-o Catholic! And a killjoy!"

I nodded and rolled my eyes, agreeing that my empathic thoughts were counter-productive for the situation.

I continued my tale. "After a couple of minutes, a shade goes down on the window and you have to insert another coin. I pulled out another pound coin, but it dropped to the floor. When I went to pick it up, the floor was this gooey mess of latex condoms and god knows what. I left the coin and tried to imagine how I would ever sanitize my hand from touching all of this gooey muck! A blow torch, perhaps? I just wanted to plunge it in alcohol for a few hours to thoroughly disinfect it."

Bob and I laughed, and then he asked me to continue my earlier story, "So, what happened in Thailand?"

"While I was in Bangkok, I decided to see a sex show in Patpong. An older buddy of mine who had been to 'Nam said that he and his friends would go to Patpong on leave for R-and-R. He said I should definitely check it out. But, when I walked around the streets a bit, it was really circus-like and guys were hustling you like crazy. I was alone in town and didn't like the idea of going around without someone to cover my back."

"Makes sense," Bob interjected. "I can relate."

"So, I talked to a concierge at my hotel, and he set me up with a limo driver who would take me to a show. The cost was minimal for the limo and driver…maybe $10 for the night and I figured this was the best way to go. I didn't have to worry about being taken advantage of by the sex show barkers who hustled the hell out of you. And, I had a ride to and from the destination. So anyway, we went to this non-descript apartment building in a back-alley and I was directed to a basement door. No signs. No markings. I wasn't sure what I was walking into. Hell, I was just doing this on the word of a limo driver I had just met. At the very least, I thought that I could get drugged and robbed."

"Did you chicken out?"

"No, I went inside the door and there was an old woman behind a folding table with a simple metal cash box. She told me the admission price, I paid her and she directed me down the hall to a curtain. A doorman by the curtain pulled it back and I went into this small bar with tables and a stage with a walkway. Like for a fashion show."

I continued. "The place was practically empty, just minutes before show time, which made me feel really uncomfortable. So, I went to the bar to grab a drink. I asked the bartender why it was so empty and he said not to worry, there was a busload of Korean businessmen arriving at any moment. So I ordered a Coke and carefully watched the bartender as he opened the bottle and brought it over. The bottle never left my sight, so I knew it was safe to drink."

"Smart," Bob said. "Ultra-paranoid, but safe."

"*Exactly.*"

"So, what was the show like?"

"Well, before it started, I had finished my drink and needed to pee. So I went to the men's room and to one of about a half dozen urinals. There was a door to the right of me and I guessed it was for cleaning supplies for the restroom. I was in the middle of my leak when the door suddenly opened. About ten scantily dressed women exited from what I thought was their dressing room and walk through the men's room, and out into the bar. I had seen women in co-ed bathrooms in Paris, but this was a new one!"

"So, how was the show?" Bob seemed anxious to hear a few details.

"Several strippers paraded up and down the walkway, but they weren't very enthusiastic, just going through the motions. They'd finish and walk off. I guessed they were the warm up acts. Then, there were a few *specialty* acts. One young woman shot ping pong balls from her vagina while squatting, and bounced them into a shot glass."

"Sounds like a fraternity party game."

"That would be one popular fraternity, Bob." I continued, "The poor girl couldn't do it the first couple of tries. She'd squat, force out a ball and it would bounce and miss the shot glass. She kept missing and then she kept chasing after the ping-pong ball around the stage. She'd then clean it in a glass of water, re-insert it and then try again. I felt bad for her and cheered her on. There were some Korean businessmen nearby who were not impressed and didn't clap once. She finally completed the trick and then exited the stage.

"Then this woman, who was old enough to have entertained our boys back in the days of Vietnam, came out and drew pictures on large white sheets of butcher paper using a big, bold poster marker she inserted inside her. She'd squat over the paper and, using the marker, draw a beach scene with a sunset. Like a picture postcard. She'd give it away to someone near the stage." I shook my head and added, "Weird."

After a slight pause, I continued, "Another woman shot these little bananas from between her legs."

"A pussy cannon," Bob interjected with great enthusiasm.

"Something like that. All of us in the audience just tried to not get hit by one of the projectiles." I shuddered as I recalled the image. "Yuck."

"So, was the show what you expected?"

"When I thought about a sex show, or a bed show, I imagined live male-female intercourse. Which, as it turned out, was what the Main Act was all about."

"Finally!" Bob joked, "I thought you'd never get to the point. Geez, Nejman. Finish your story so we can get back to me."

"Yeah, sorry. So sorry. I didn't intend to go off on such a tangent," I was genuinely apologetic, knowing I had ventured off on a lengthy detour.

"To make a long story, short. Wait! Too late," Bob teased.

"So this tall Amer-Asian male came out and he was probably six-feet tall and muscular with this beautiful, but tiny Thai woman. They were both naked and performed a choreographed dance, like an elaborate ballet. At some point, he inserted himself inside her and then they slowly shifted into a wide variety of positions. I couldn't believe how he kept erect the whole time." I thought for a moment and continued, "No problem with stage fright."

"Or performance anxiety," Bob chimed in.

"It was very beautifully done, although without a single moan or climax. After a brief performance which took all of a few minutes, they took a bow and that was that."

"And no problems? You didn't get drugged or robbed?"

"Nope, all went well and I hopped back in the limo and back to the hotel."

"Did they have any souvenirs? I'm sure the T-shirts had to be fun."

"Sadly, no. No souvenir shop."

"Too bad," Bob smirked. "A missed marketing opportunity. You could have sent home a postcard back home to mom. She'd be so proud."

Without acknowledging his comment, I knew I had to get the conversation back on track, "So, where were we? You were worried about getting drugged as you were driving to Ed's house in the middle of the night…"

"Yeah," Bob nodded, ready to finally pick-up where he had left off. "I was really excited pulling up to his house. It was gorgeous. And as I get out of my car, I think, please god, don't let him be wearing beige," Bob laughed at his one great concern. "So of course, Edward answers the door…in beige! But, he's a glorious vision in beige."

Bob began to describe the scene with the same giddiness a child would recall his first encounter with Santa Claus on Christmas morning. "He's a six-foot tall, blonde *shiksa*, every Jew's fantasy. A young David Hockney. And, he's in these beautiful beige linen pants, like something out of *The Great Gatsby*. He was a professor of English Lit at Manhattan College and he's a published author and poet. His favorite book was *Ulysses* by James Joyce, which is my favorite book of all-time!"

"A sign," I said, my eyes widening.

"Then, somehow we get on the topic of key lime pie. And we both love key lime pie. And, he has a key lime tree in his yard."

"Really?" I looked impressed. "How cool is that? Another sign."

"And you know, a psychic in Rancho Cucamonga had predicted my meeting Ed." Bob continued. "She said, 'you'll meet a man, he'll come to your show, and you'll know.' "

"You'll know?"

"He's *it!!*" Bob said with a big, toothy smile.

"Ah! But, the psychic missed the key lime connection though, huh?"

"No key lime, but she predicted the situation. I met Ed, he came to my Chicago show, and that was the turning point. I knew!"

"Oh yeah, your show at the David Leonardis Gallery. Quite the coming out party as I recall."

"Wait! I'm getting ahead of myself," Bob said. "Linear storytelling has never been my strength. Anyway, we meet and…"

"Talk key lime pie," I interjected.

"Talk key lime pie, and I'm, well, more than interested. I mean, he's charming, well read, and he had this wonderfully twisted sense of humor."

"Ah! Apparently, a trait we all share," I said. "Very cool."

Bob glanced over at me, "Right." I wasn't sure how he meant that.

"So, it's late and I gotta get back to the house. So, Edward invites me back for breakfast the next morning."

"So, he was a perfect gentleman? No *roofies*? No psychotic behavior?" I paused and exhibited mock despair. "I'm disappointed. Where's the tension and intrigue in that? Sounds pretty Rock Hudson – Doris Day to me."

"Well I was relieved. We had a promising blind date that was to be continued."

"So the next day you guys meet over bagels?"

"Better! Cheese omelets," Bob said with a smile. "But, I'm feeling insecure and a tad neurotic, so I sense this need to bring my art portfolio to…" he paused slightly and gave a sheepish grin, "…prove I'm a talented guy."

"Understandable. Early date. He's rich and successful. You want to show you have much to offer." We're on the same page, I assured Bob.

"Right. So before the orange juice, I eagerly say, 'do you want to see my portfolio?' " Bob said with a half-smile and cringed, as he couldn't believe he made such a lame, insecure faux pas. "I don't recall Ed's actual response, but it was barely a nod because I *whip* out my portfolio!" Bob motions like he pulled out a huge portfolio.

"NO!" I started to laugh. "Smooth move, dude!"

"Ed told me later, he's thinking, god, please don't let it be black velvet."

We both laughed.

Bob continued, "But to my great relief, he *loves* my work.

So, we eat our omelets and he surprises me with a homemade key lime pie that is to die for! We talk for a couple of hours, and then we agree to head out to this nearby gay restaurant in Palm Springs for lunch where we have this great, spirited, spontaneous conversation, with this amazing clarity. We didn't have to work for dialogue or topics; it all flowed naturally."

"Sounds impressive," I said, with genuine sincerity. "Talk about a great connection! It was meant to be," I nodded, showing my support.

"So, we came to his place, made out on the sofa, and quickly moved to the bedroom." Bob paused and gave me a really big grin. "Ed was hung like a horse! I had scored the Brass Ring: tall, blonde, brilliant, hung, and a bottom!"

"That's *way* too much information," I said as I put out my right hand like a stop sign. Smiling, I added, "But I appreciate your enthusiasm."

I hadn't spent much time with Edward, maybe a short conversation or two at the gallery. Now it will be a bit awkward to talk with him and not think about my new insider information.

Bob went on to tell me that Edward — a successful teacher, author and poet — was also a very astute businessman who made very wise investments. He had royalty checks not only from his own published books, but also from his mother, songwriter Sylvia Dee. She had penned several musical gems in the 1950s and '60s including: "Too Young," a hit for Nat King Cole; "Bring Me Sunshine" which was very popular in the UK; "The End of the World" which was made famous by Skeeter Davis and featured in the movie soundtracks; and several songs for Elvis Presley's films *Blue Hawaii* and *Speedway*. Between royalties and investments, Bob shared that Edward was very wealthy.

It was getting late and we were both hungry. Omaha, Nebraska was only minutes away, so we started to look for lodging signs and the friendly Holiday Inn logo to head us to the perfect roadside trinity: clean, cheap and close.

We pulled off the road at 8 p.m., nine-and-a-half hours and

470 miles after we had begun. We were both very satisfied and impressed with our first day's progress. As we pulled into the parking lot, I couldn't help but notice the fresh graveyard of insects that had accumulated on our windshield. I made a mental note to deal with it in the morning when we gassed-up.

We went into the hotel lobby where a white-haired clerk behind the counter greeted Bob and he secured our room.

Just as promised, Bob covered the cost of hotel and gas; all I had to do was take care of my meals. More than fair and a very tidy deal.

As we walked our bags to our room, I opened up to Bob, "A few days ago, I mentioned to another close friend that we were going on this road trip and how I want to make a change in my life. I want to commit to one person and create a life together. And my friend says to me, 'A leopard can't change his spots. You are who you are and there's no changing your core being, your primal self. You will forever be Peter Pan and continue to avoid commitment.' " As I said those words, I felt as if I was cursed to live a destiny that was already set in motion. I continued, "As I thought about it, I got really depressed. I'm getting older and I don't want to end up alone."

"Yep," Bob said. "Some day your looks will disappear and you'll be old and alone, unless you change. Such is life." His delivery was light and playful, as if to stress that I shouldn't get too bummed out about the inevitable.

"Gee, thanks for the reassurance. You're a real pal," I chuckled.

"I'm always here to help," he smiled. "Don't worry, I'm sure there's someone out there who will mop up your drool."

We walked up a flight of stairs to the second floor and room 221. Bob inserted our room key into the lock, opened the door, and I trailed behind.

"I read this John Cougar Mellencamp quote the other day," I began as I looked about the room, deciding which bed to sleep in. "He said that men shouldn't marry until they're 40. They're lousy at it until then." I thought for a moment as I placed my bag on the second bed, the one closest to the bathroom. "The way I look at it, I've just turned 40, so the timing is right for me to make a change in my life." Then with confidence, I declared, "I think there's still time for me to change my spots."

Chapter Eleven

Day Two on the road:
Omaha, Nebraska to Golden, Colorado

I woke up with an offensive, parasitic earworm playing in my brain: "Come Sail Away" by Styx. The brief exposure yesterday morning from the radio was enough to deposit this pop-tune insect egg into my brain, which had now hatched into its larva stage. I needed a dose of real rock'n'roll to exterminate it before it drove me insane! Unfortunately for me, it was Sunday, so the celebration of pop music was on most stations: *Casey's Top 40.* Casey Kasem's cheesy deejay delivery showcased mainstream pop radio hits along with a sappy "long-distance dedication." So, instead of a cure for my earworm this would only *further* imbed other selections of pop tripe into my brain!

As I turned on the radio near my bed, Hanson's "Mmmbop" was playing, an innocuous song that ruled the charts with a dominating eight-week run at #1 that year, along with forgettable hits by The Cardigans, Jewel, and Chumbawamba. Casey provided chart trivia between songs, as

I tried to wake up and prepare for another day. I desperately struggled with the tuner to find some Classic Rock, but failed. There were only religious talk shows, boring local public service programming, and an Oldies station that seemed to broadcast an all-Perry Como, all-the-time format. That was it. That was all. So, *Casey's Top 40* was the tepid victor from a field of lame choices.

Bob was all dressed and ready to leave as I rolled over and focused my eyes. He sat in a chair staring at me, a wordless plea for me to get up and get going.

Nature called, so my first priority was a bathroom break in our safe, clean bathroom. I mention *safe* because it will undoubtedly be a superb option to the usually disgusting public men's rooms in the restaurants, gas stations and rest areas we would most likely frequent later in the day. Men immediately understand this. However, if you are a woman reading this memoir, take my word that a great many roadside toilets resemble the "most disgusting toilet in all of Scotland" scene in the 1996 movie *Trainspotting*. If you haven't seen the movie, imagine the most vile, smelly, germ-infested toilet you can, and then note that there's no toilet paper and the slime on the floor is moving.

It was morning and I needed to talk to Mr. Hankey.

'I need to use the bathroom," I declared and turned up the radio. I hate when people can hear my bathroom activity, so I needed to drown out any telltale sound effects.

"Zolzein gezunt," Bob said in Yiddish. "Be well," he translated when I looked perplexed by his comment.

Closing the bathroom door, I took a seat and mercifully found instant success. This was a huge relief for me. No pain, no strain. Usually in the morning, after breakfast and a piping hot cup of coffee, I have a brief window of maybe 20 minutes to take the Browns to the Super Bowl. But today, without the aid of any outside stimuli, I was good to go. Regularity, good; constipation, not so good.

I washed up, brushed my teeth, zipped up my faux leather travel toiletries bag, and ran a damp hand through my hair. I glanced at myself in the mirror, under the harsh fluorescent light, and determined that I looked a bit rough, but presentable.

Struggling in the dimly lit room, it took a few moments to locate my clothes near the bed and dress quickly. To save time, neither of us bothered to shave or shower that second morning. We simply put on the clothes we wore the previous day, re-packed our bags, checked out, and left in search of breakfast.

I began to write in my notebook journal, not only jotting down practical information about daily mileage, travel costs, and stopping points, but also my thoughts and observations, especially highlights of our road trip therapy sessions. There were new lists; good lists; helpful lists!

By 8 a.m. on Sunday, May 25, we were having breakfast at the Garden Café in Omaha, just down the street from our Holiday Inn. The previous day, we had driven from 10:30 a.m. until 8 p.m., and made just short of 500 miles, according to the odometer number I scratched down in the journal. A nine-and-a-half hour first day on the road is brutal, but it does help to build endurance. I sensed that today's driving goals would probably meet or exceed yesterday's totals, unless we began to take advantage of opportunities to stop and enjoy the trip more. Considering the painfully boring, flat terrain we covered during Day One as we drove through Illinois and Iowa, it only made sense to drive long and hard to get closer to the hilly, mountainous beauty of Colorado.

As I looked around the restaurant, I observed a *real* lack of diversity: No people of color whatsoever. Everyone was white, with blue eyes and blond hair. It felt like we were in Sweden, not Omaha. For me, Nebraska seemed bleak. It was flat, cloudy, foggy, and never-ending. The Purgatory of America. Bob was not very talkative during the meal, but that was all right with me, as I wanted to jot down at least a few bullet points to document our trip for future reference. I was in a list mode. I looked outside the window and it was dreary. The sunny day we had yesterday was long gone and the threat of rain loomed ominously in the sky.

After a breakfast of eggs, toast, orange juice and coffee, we felt somewhat rested and a bit "road ripe" from the previous day's travel. *Thank goodness for scented deodorant*, I thought.

We stopped for gas at a nearby station. While Bob filled the tank, I worked diligently to scrape the bug remains off the windshield. Gross bits of wings and guts stuck to the glass as I tried several times to squeegee it clean, but the bug juice proved to be challenging to remove. Eventually, after several tries, the window shined, a fresh slate for a new selection of flies, wasps, and assorted winged pests.

Within minutes, we returned to the open road. Our stomachs and gas tank were full, plus we had hot coffee to go, and a fairly reasonable radio station playing Classic Rock from the Sixties. Life was good!

Bob took the first driving shift as I got comfortable in the passenger seat. Had I wanted perfection I would have had a sexy brunette at my side. Unfortunately for me, my partner was Nathan Lane, not Diane Lane.

Bob was perky and I was sitting dead. I was not a morning person. Best scenario: We'd start our day at 10 a.m. and ease into the world drinking coffee until noon. It was barely 9 a.m. and far too early to have a deep conversation. I studied the road atlas for 20 minutes, looking at where we'd been and what was in store for us the next few days. As I reviewed the previous day's route, my eyes happened upon Normal, Illinois and nearby Carlock. I snickered to myself.

Bob sat up in his seat. "What's so funny?"

Even though it was cloudy, Bob had dark sunglasses on to shield his eyes from the unwanted light of the day.

"I can't help but wonder what was on the minds of some of these city founders when they named their communities. I mean, Normal, Illinois. Really? Could any name be more bland?"

"I once knew this androgynous, gigantic gender-fucker named Billie; this Bowie-esque character from outer space.

Face paint and all. He modeled for one of my paintings…in fact, it was in my last gallery show. He was from Normal. Go *figger.*"

"Love the irony." My index finger marked a location on the Illinois map of the road atlas, "There's a place in Illinois called Carlock. Like Muffler was already taken and no other car part was available."

"I think there's a Boring, Oregon," Bob said. "How awful is that! Hell, I'd want nothing more than to escape *Bore-ring!*"

I countered, "What about French Lick, Indiana? It sounds like a sexual service you'd order from a bordello menu." I imitated a proper English gentleman, "Yes, I think a French Lick would be jolly good today, what!" I continued to look at the atlas. "Or what about places named Fairview. The town founder actually looked over the terrain and said, well this is not a *great* view, just a *fair* view. That's what we'll call this town: Fairview. Talk about low self-esteem."

"Or, hyper-critical," Bob offered. "So, what's in your journal? I saw you writing in it earlier."

"I'm keeping a record of our trip. You know…daily progress, observations, lists, this and that. I even have my 'musts' list."

"Musts?" Bob chuckled. "As in things we *must* do?"

"Exactly," I grinned, with just a smidgeon of enthusiasm; it was still too early to be cheery.

"That is so *you.*"

I couldn't tell if it was a compliment or an insult, but it didn't really matter to me. I had a short list of *musts* — or goals — that I wanted to check off as went along our merry way to Palm Springs. "So, you want to hear the list?"

"Sure. Can't wait," Bob said with a grin as he turned down the radio. Again, I couldn't determine if he was being sincere or facetious. Most days I felt like Bob was the Enigma machine and I was Alan Turing constantly trying to break his code.

I opened my journal and found my *Must List* on the second page. I glanced at my first item and shared it with Bob, "Well, since we're taking Route 80 to 76 to Denver and picking up

Route 70, maybe we could stop by Rocky Mountain National Park. I think it's about 90 minutes north of Denver."

"Hmm," he shrugged. "I don't know. That's three hours round trip. We can see how we feel about it, as we get closer. You've been there before?"

"In 1976, the Bicentennial, Candy and I drove cross-country and camped up on Longs Peak during a horrible rainstorm which caused the Big Thompson Flood.

"As I recall, it was Colorado's Centennial so they had climbers on every mountaintop; many were stranded for hours after the rains; it was pretty scary. Candy and I barely got out of the area because of mudslides and boulders in the road. We saw quite a bit of the park before the storm though, and it was breathtaking. I'd love to spend some time there."

Bob just mumbled quizzically, "So, why go there again?"

I pulled out one of my throwaway cameras from my duffel bag and said with great zeal, "So I can capture our Kodak Moments!"

My fervor was met with an indifferent, "We'll see."

"Oh," I said, mildly disappointed, but remaining optimistic. "Or, we could stop by Boulder. It's only 30 miles or so from Denver. That's not so far and it's really a nice place to stop for a bite to eat."

Again, I hit Bob's Wall of Apathy, and a practically inaudible grunt.

"What?" I said

"Uh-huh, cool. Sure," Bob said as if I had declared that I had wanted to see the World's Biggest Ball of Twine.

"Well, once we get to Utah, there are lots of places to stop, like Arches National Park or Zion. They're both near I-70, so they'd be convenient stops."

No reaction from Bob.

"And then of course, we drive through Vegas! Maybe we can stop and take in a show or at least walk The Strip."

Bob thought for a moment and smiled slightly as he said, "That has potential. I like that: titty shows, buffets, and I think there's a Liberace museum, too. How groovy!"

I wasn't a fan of Liberace, but I guess I could hit The Strip while Bob amused himself at the museum. None of my choices seemed to spark him, so I looked down at my journal, and pretended to read the next several options, creating a few fantasy stops of my own.

"Well, there's this town near Vegas that pays tribute to Michael Jackson by only allowing people named Michael to reside within the town's limits. Surprisingly, the town is called Jeff. "

Bob grimaced and barely registered a chuckle on the imaginary Laugh-o-Meter in my mind, so I vowed to myself to at least get him to guffaw or chortle before the day's end.

"Also near Vegas are Uncle Larry's House of Tweed, which is just kitty-corner to The Wonderful World of Navel Lint Laundromat and Museum. Any interest? I think a souvenir keepsake T-shirt from either establishment would be well worth the effort."

Bob fought a smile, but he was losing the battle, not wanting to give me the satisfaction of getting him to laugh.

"Or, we could check out this historical church, Our Lady of Anal Vapors."

"I think you mean *hysterical*," he snickered. "Enough already! You're ruining my angelic image of you as an altar boy!"

It felt good to goof around and break up the tediousness of the seemingly endless, flat asphalt strip of road we were stuck on. The humor was admittedly weak, but I was desperate to inject some lightheartedness into what seemed like an utterly miserable day.

As Bob drove, I pulled out one of my disposable Kodak cameras and took a couple of shots of him behind the wheel, as well as a few pictures of the view from my passenger- side vantage point. As the documentarian of our twosome, I felt it was important to record a little bit about each day, both in my journal and with photography.

We reached North Platte around noon and decided to stop for lunch and a chance to stretch our legs.

The view outside our vehicle had been static and boring, farms and fields, telephone poles and power lines for hours. The lone visual highlight was when we could see the Platte River and the rolling hills leading to it. The weather continued to be cloudy and gray throughout the state. There was an occasional spritz of rain on the windshield, just enough to warrant the use of the wipers but not enough to flush off the new bug innards glued to the glass. We headed toward a distant sky that looked more troubled and ominous.

I got behind the wheel and started my shift driving.

Chapter Twelve

The Bob and Ed Story

Programming on the radio was erratic. Sundays were tricky. There were probably a handful stations to choose from and nothing we heard was good. I turned the tuning knob, trying to score the Stones or Beatles, but found only lame Country pop and fiery sermons. We needed something to fill the time and take our minds off the miles of monotony. I broke the silence, wanting to learn more about the beginning of Bob's relationship with Ed.

"So, where did we leave off on the Bob and Ed Story? I think we had established that you met and, if this were heaven…" I drew a level imaginary line in front of me, and then pointed to a spot two inches above it. "Then, this was your relationship. You were both in a state of bliss. I think you had shared your portfolio and a home-made key lime pie."

Bob smiled fondly as he remembered where he was with the story. I could see he was deeply in love. "And I grabbed the Brass Ring!"

"Yes, I recall," I said, although there was related imagery I wished I could forget.

"Soon after Ed and I met, I had my show at the David Leonardis Gallery in Chicago."

"Right. The gallery was in the heart of Wicker Park. Jennifer and I were there! Edward approached her when I was in the bathroom and said he was your lover and that we should come visit the two of you in Palm Springs," I said.

Bob corrected, "Ed said he was my lover — a millionaire— — and that you must come stay at the house."

"Yep. When she told me that, I was stunned, because I had no idea you were gay."

"The signs were there," he said. "I guess I shouldn't expect that you would have known."

"I just thought you were quirky. You had three kids and a wife after all. You couldn't be gay."

"Well, he outed me to everyone. He did me a favor actually. It was our first romantic weekend together. We had a room at the Grand Hyatt in Chicago and Paula stayed home in Palm Desert. Edward bought a couple of my paintings from the show, the one with me and Mother Theresa as well as the one of a young Oscar Wilde reclining on a couch."

"Mother Theresa? Wasn't that the photo that I took of you on Venice Beach? You stood between two posters of Mother Theresa at some vendor's stand. I think I called it 'Saint and Sinner Sandwich,' " I recalled. Bob had moved from Los Angeles to Desert Hot Springs and I visited for a week, which included photographically documenting his home in the desert and a trip we took one afternoon to Venice Beach.

"I love that image. I hand-painted over the photo. Outrageous. Colorful," Bob complimented his own work. "So, Ed buys the two paintings. And, he gets plastered on Tanqueray." There was a pause and Bob started to sound upset, "It was my mother all over again. Once again, I'm relegated to being a caretaker!"

I hadn't had very many interactions with Bob's mother, Millie, but the few I had were a very mixed bag. Sometimes she would be cordial and interesting to talk with, while other times she would be totally inebriated and hostile.

"God, I remember the time we were at a party near your place on Armitage. One of your friends threw it and Millie was with us."

"Oh yeah, she was plastered barely an hour into the party," he recalled with a laugh.

"She was so funny!" I mimicked her rough, raspy truck-driver-like voice, "'Rah-bert! Rah-bert!'"

Bob laughed at my spot-on impersonation. I continued, "She was falling down drunk, so a few of us removed her from the party and took her to your car."

"I think we had a person on each of her legs and arms. Four of us lugging an old drunken Jewish woman down a never-ending, steep flight of stairs," Bob added.

The image in my mind reminded me of the insanity of the situation and I began to howl with laughter as I recalled each detail of that evening.

"I was laughing so hard, I thought I'd pee in my pants. I think we tried to get her down the back porch stairs, but they were too narrow and her body couldn't be manipulated to make it work. So we had to re-group and go down the front stairs."

"It was so icy and cold, I thought for sure we were going to bob-sled her down the stairs," Bob said, and it reminded me of the incredibly slick conditions of that wintery Chicago evening.

"And, then we finally get her to your car and put her in the passenger seat and I'm like, 'Good seeing you, Bob, take care.' And you say, 'I'm not leaving. I'm going back to the party.' 'But what about your mom?' I ask. And you say, 'Who's going to steal an old Jewish woman?'"

"I said that?" Bob was laughing harder now, not realizing that he was so flippant about his mother's well-being that evening. "Am I the good son, or what?"

I wiped my eyes as they teared up from laughter.

"I don't think I ever told you this, but one time I took her to a movie after she had had a few cocktails. So, we're watching the coming attractions, probably 15 minutes of them, and she announced," Bob imitated her raspy voice to the tee, "'I don't like this movie, take me home!' "

We both laughed some more. Initially, I had thought Bob was mean to his mom, but I began to see how her drunkenness really made having a normal mother-son relationship impossible for them. It was obvious that he had to be the adult around her, not only monitoring her wild, careless behavior, but also dealing with the humiliation of her acting out in public, especially amongst his friends and colleagues. I think it was healthy for Bob to be able to laugh about his mom and her on-going bout with alcoholism, as it was certainly beyond his ability to control her behavior.

After awhile, I decided to return to our original discussion, "So, wait, where were we in your story?" I thought for a moment, trying to recall where we had left off. "You were outed at the Leonardis Gallery Show and Ed bought a couple of your paintings."

"Right," Bob started up where he left off. "So a month or so later, it's Christmas with the Fischers in Palm Desert. Ed brings over his two kids, Elizabeth and Christopher, and of course, there's Paula and my kids, Aaron, Jarrett, and Morgan. The whole experience is polite, if not a tad awkward, and then, Paula gets her first clue that I'm gay."

Bob paused as a dramatic effect, urging me to listen closely. Then he said discreetly, as if being careful that no one else would hear, "She buys me a bottle of my favorite cologne, and Ed also buys me the same cologne, but a bigger bottle!"

"Oops!" My eyes grow wide as I acknowledged the faux pas.

"Then, I tell her that Edward is my benefactor and taking me to Australia for a couple of weeks to check out their gallery scene. At the airport, after Paula and I say our goodbyes, Ed gets down on one knee and proposes. Of course, I accepted and we went off to Australia."

"Wow! He didn't waste any time. Obviously, he knew you were the one for him!" *I guess when you know, you know,* I thought to myself. Here I had been in relationships for months, and even years, and struggled with determining if my partner was the right person for me, to commit to her. Yet, Edward was so taken with Bob, he proposed within weeks of meeting him. I was happy for Bob, to find someone who truly loved and admired him. But, I was curious, "So, when did you come out to Paula and tell her your big news?"

"Well, Ed and I got back at the end of January and I had planned to tell Paula on Valentine's Day."

"Roses are red, violets are blue; I'm gay and no longer attracted to you?"

"Something like that," Bob continued. "But, when I get back from Australia, she corners me and is insistent that something's going on. So under the pressure of her questioning me, I blurt out, 'Yes, I'm gay, I want a divorce, and I'm leaving right now.' "

"Poor Paula. That must have been rough." All of the time I had known Paula, I had observed her to be a very sweet, thoughtful and friendly person. She had always supported Bob and his art, as well as being a loving mother to her three children.

"I felt bad, but not enough to stay. I loved Edward. That was no tough choice. It was simple."

"True," I agreed.

"Shortly after all this, I painted a portrait of Edward and he's wearing these rose-colored glasses," Bob said. I nod as I recall the specific painting he is describing. "Those aren't his glasses, though. They're mine," Bob said with great clarity. "I truly love Edward, but he's an alcoholic. I stay because 65 % of the time, life is great and he's not physically abusive. And, I can just do my art and wake up next to the man I love."

"As a child of an alcoholic, maybe that has something to do with your being drawn to him." Somehow I needed a reason, but sometimes there are no lists or reasons.

Bob nodded, "Okay."

The last hour or so was quite an emotional roller-coaster and we were now beginning a downward dip. In an attempt to lighten the mood, I offered, "Hey you two are happy together, and that's all that's important." As I heard myself say that, I felt like a writer for some lame Hallmark card.

"Yep" Bob said, forcing a smile.

With that, our road trip therapy session for the day came to a close as our rolling confessional continued down the highway.

Lost in discussion, I hadn't paid attention to the progress we made as we had just crossed the Colorado border as we hopped on Route 76 toward Denver, having just left Nebraska and Route 80. The weather was constantly changing for the last half hour or so, from cloudy and rain, to sunny, and then back to rain again. The upcoming leg of the journey included a driving rainstorm, and once that let up, we witnessed a dust devil in the dry, flat plains between Sterling and Fort Morgan. It was strange to witness such diverse weather conditions within a matter of minutes.

Driving through the bad weather was more demanding and tiring than our earlier cruising under sunny skies, but the view of the majestic Rocky Mountains growing on the horizon, kept us motivated to continue on.

It was almost 6 p.m. when we pulled into the parking lot of a Holiday Inn in Golden, Colorado. The warm, safe and reassuring glow of the yellow and green sign was a welcoming beacon as we parked the truck and slowly walked into the lobby.

I couldn't help but note how every major exit on the highway was starting to look alike. Endless signs with corporate logos for McDonald's, Arby's, Wendy's, Amoco, Texaco, Taco Bell, and the like, lined the main drag of each exit for as far as the eye could see. We could be in southern Illinois, central Ohio, or eastern Nebraska. It was all the same. I had a feeling this homogenous existence was the result of all the constant change in our lives as a society. With so much change, people seek consistency; we look for the norm. So as we travel, there's always a safe, reassuring option with a familiar logo for both eating standard American fare and staying at cozy, family-friendly hotels.

Bob and I checked-in, located our room, dropped off our bags, and then walked down the street to a well-lit Denny's. As Bob perused the menu, I started to jot down the day's progress in my journal. It was the end of the day, May 25, and we had travelled about eight-and-a-half hours and some 550 miles from Omaha to Golden. We had exceeded the previous day's total mileage by 50 miles, and I proudly reported our achievement to Bob with all of the zeal of a sixth-grader knowing the right answer and waving his right arm to get the teacher's attention and approval.

"Great! Tomorrow, I'm sure we'll make Utah," he said as he studied the daily specials without looking up.

"Utah?" I said with more than a hint of surprise. "Aren't we going to explore some of the Denver area? Shoot up to Boulder or go hiking in the Rockies?"

"Wait, don't tell me. Those are *musts*, right," he said, playfully teasing me as he looked up from the menu. "I hadn't really thought about it," he continued. His eyes looked red and tired, his face a bit washed out. "I guess we can see how we feel in the morning and decide."

Fair enough I thought, but his lack of enthusiasm was more than a subtle hint of foreshadowing for what I should expect the next morning. I fully anticipated that we'd be hitting the road and heading west, with no hikes or tourist stops. No distractions on this leg of the journey. No Kodak Moments. He had lied to me!

As I stared at the menu I began to think, *one must calculate which battles are worth fighting.* Since I had already spent time in both Denver and Rocky Mountain National Park, this was not one of the fights I needed to address.

I had never been to Utah and there were several options coming up, such as Arches National Park or Zion National Park, that were non-negotiable for me; we would definitely be stopping for them. Without lingering on the disappointment, I nodded toward Bob with a smile and quickly made a decision to have *brinner*; that is, breakfast for dinner. Eggs, ham and toast, with a side of pancakes sounded really good to me. Bob agreed. We flagged down our waitress, and ordered our brinner.

As we enjoyed our food, I began to make plans for the following day. So far, Bob was used to getting his way, but I knew that this was about to change.

Chapter Thirteen

Day Three on the road:
Golden, Colorado to Cedar City, Utah

Some days, the atmosphere seems more dense and gravity heavier. On days like those, one's joints and muscles have a dull ache and it feels like one moves in slow motion, like one is walking through an aquarium. This is how Day Three of our road trip started for me. No one had to tell me it was a Monday. It felt like a Monday. Just the simple act of getting out of bed and trudging to the bathroom, a mere three feet from my bed, seemed to take all of the energy I could muster. The long hours on the road were taking their toll on me and, rather than hop back into the vehicle and head West, my body yearned for another few hours of deep, coma-like sleep and a leisurely morning in front of some brainless television shows while sipping coffee. Instead, Bob was once again already dressed and ready to hit the road. No lingering for me, it was time to go.

He sat in a chair staring out the window, lost in thought I presumed as he watched the sun just begin to peak over the horizon. Perhaps he wasn't lost in thought, but capable of sleeping with his eyes open. I couldn't tell for sure. Several questions occurred to me as I pulled back the covers: How early did he get up? When did he sleep? Was he superhuman?

"Mornin', Bob," I said in a very deep, sleepy register, my voice all raspy and gritty. I didn't think my comment projected very far outside my body, but Bob reacted with a similar greeting as I shuffled slowly to the bathroom.

I groaned a bit as I stood in front of the toilet and emptied my bladder. Out of the corner of my eye, I saw myself in the mirror, with my hamster-head hairstyle, squinty eyes and unshaven face. I had crawled out from the wreckage, yet desperately needed to return to the quiet comfort of my bed to convalesce. My eyes slowly began to shut as I waited for my stream of urine to subside.

"C'mon Sleeping Beauty, breakfast, and then the road!" Bob growled, startling me back into sudden consciousness. *So, much for easing into the day,* I thought.

"Gimme a minute, will ya!" I hollered back, not unlike a younger version of myself responding to my mom urging me to get ready for school. I started to run the faucet so I could splash cold water on my face. Blindly, I cleaned and gently placed my contacts into my eyes. It took awhile for me to focus clearly. It's not that they were not clean of smudges, it was just that my eyesight was still hazy and out of focus. After several blinks and then concentrating on a few distant objects in the room, I realized all was well. Next, I brushed my teeth, sprayed deodorant under my pits, and paused for a moment to stare at my hair. What a disaster! It desperately needed to be washed, but there was no time for a shower. So, I wet my hands under the water, ran them through my hair, and blow-dried it out so that it looked somewhat presentable. Again, I glanced at the mirror and determined that this will have to do for now.

As I left the bathroom, I spied my clothes from the previous day hanging on a chair near a table. The shirt was two days old and ripe from sweat, so I grabbed a clean one from my bag. I pulled out my favorite black T-shirt, which was worn and comfortable, and put it on. My cargo shorts still looked fairly clean and I slipped those on as well, expecting that they'd be good for the week.

"Denny's?"

"Fine." My response was barely audible as I pulled on my socks and began to tie my gym shoes. Before I'd even completed this task though, Bob was already out the door and walking away. I grabbed my wallet, wristwatch, and a clean handkerchief, and quickly followed behind.

"What's the rush?" I stumbled out our hotel door and slammed it behind me; hoping Bob had the only key with him.

"I just want to get home. I really miss Ed."

As I fastened my watch on to my wrist, I notice that it was barely 7:30 a.m. This road trip was technically a vacation for me, and while on vacation, it was far more common for me to come home at 7:30 in the morning, than it was for me to get up and be functioning at this ungodly hour. Bob's pace was swift, and I barely managed to stay within a few steps behind him. Like a runner in a marathon, I just kept in stride with him knowing that the restaurant door would slow him down and I'd make my move to catch up. As we walked, I couldn't help but notice his attire. He was wearing purple shorts with images of white bunnies with "X"s for eyes, so I supposed they were stoned, and a tight white tank top with a bold American flag on the front.

"Interesting fashion choices," I said.

"I'm going *full-stealth* today," he said smiling.

"Full stealth?"

"Yep, I'm going to just blend in with everyone else."

"Only if you're in a room full of Richard Simmons wannabes," I said under my breath, but well within earshot of my target.

Bob's idea of what the average American wore from a casual perspective was amusing, if not mind-boggling to me. I guess I should have expected this from a guy who actually made a vest out of stiff shag carpeting when he was in junior high, an attempt to imitate a vest he saw worn by Sonny Bono on television; cool idea, weak execution.

Breakfast seemed like a blur as we quickly ordered, received our food, and each gulped down a piping hot cup of coffee within minutes of sitting at our booth. Bob had ordered an egg white veggie omelet with lots of hot sauce, substituting a fruit cup for the hash browns, a specialty order that required our waitress to make a series of notations on her pad. For me, a simple "number two."

Rather than talk, we focused on eating our food as we cleaned our plates faster than a cheetah running the 50-yard dash while on crystal meth. The meal, although low in fiber, stimulated my system and I suddenly realized I needed to run back to the room. Bob thought it was odd that I was squeamish about using the public restroom at the restaurant, but I didn't care; this was a basic, non-negotiable need. All I required was a window of ten minutes of quiet time to sit down – in private – and focus on my personal needs, plus a few minutes of time to commute back to the room.

"Listen, give me a ten-minute head start," I said as I got up from our booth. "Then, stroll back to the room. I promise we can get going as soon as I'm done. Why don't you relax and the read the paper or something?"

Bob sipped his coffee and looked for the waitress to get our check. I looked at him for a response.

"Go!" He flicked his wrist and motioned for me to get moving. "Take the key!" He gave me our only room key, and I assumed the message was received and agreed upon.

I ran back to our room and dashed for the bathroom. I closed the door, took a seat and tried to relax as I had hoped to finish within the allotted time. It was not unusual for me to play *Beat the Clock* with my personal habits.

No more than a minute had passed, when there was a loud knocking at the room door. *Oh no, not maid service*, I thought. Of all the bad timing! But it was not housekeeping at all as I heard Bob continue to knock and then start shouting, "Let me in!"

What the fuck! Is he serious? My window for success was

rapidly closing! I had been given the "go" for launch, but now Mission Control had suddenly terminated the assignment. I pulled up my pants and got to the door to open it.

"What are you doing?" I asked furiously. His thoughtless behavior was frustrating. "Can I not have ten fucking minutes of privacy?"

"Just do your thing, what's the big deal?"

The deal was that I needed to take care of my business first thing in the morning after breakfast, plus I hate for someone to hear my bathroom activity. I'm very self-conscious about this and it made it difficult for me to proceed. I'm sure others, like Bob, can go whenever and wherever the urge occurs, but that's just not me. We all poop and in a perfect world, we probably should have discussed this earlier in the trip. Lesson learned.

"Fine!" I said stepping away and back to the bathroom. "Just put on the TV and turn it up, will you?"

I walked back to the toilet, closed the door, took a seat and again, tried to relax. All I could concentrate on though was the absolute quiet of the room. Bob did not turn on the TV. For all I knew, he was outside the door listening, softly giggling as he mocked me.

After a minute or two, I realized that there wasn't going to be any activity for now, so I washed my hands and began to pack up for the road.

"You are such a dick!" I said to Bob as I walked out into the room. "All I ask was for ten minutes — ten fucking minutes — and you are so fucking inconsiderate and thoughtless that you have to get your way." I knocked on the dresser, imitating him knocking at the door. "My-kel! My-kel!" My delivery was in a childishly whiney voice. I dramatically paused and glared at him. "Asshole!"

Bob snickered, "What's the big deal? Take a shit already!"

It's not that easy, I thought to myself. "Forget it," I said and started to throw my things into my bag. "Let's just get on the fucking road!"

If the morning bathroom incident wasn't enough to add a

little stress to my day, all I could tune in on our radio was an innocuous, local *morning zoo* show, radio programming that was all the rage back then in most major markets.

Each substantial city in the country had a team of wacky, zany deejays who cracked jokes and performed comedy bits during morning rush hour in an attempt to lighten the mood for commuters trapped in bumper-to-bumper traffic. The on-air atmosphere was circus-like and a free-for-all, hence the *zoo* reference. Most of these shows were really lame with pun-ny jokes that were punctuated with forced laughter.

Of course, this wouldn't have been a problem if someone had secured a cassette player for our vehicle, I thought to myself while darting a killer glare at an unsuspecting Bob. We would have had several mix-tapes to choose from to help us get through this morning, but alas, that was not the case. And so I valiantly pressed onward: constipated, music-free and pummeled with bad jokes.

The morning zoo show we were listening to was more lame than most, its only redeeming quality being a fairly challenging trivia contest each hour. The station played the Rolling Stones that morning and the trivia questions were related to Mick and the boys.

After the 9 a.m. news headlines, the question was posed: "The Stones released 'Sympathy for the Devil' in December of 1968 on the album *Beggar's Banquet*. Who produced that record and went on to produce *Let it Bleed*, *Sticky Fingers*, and *Exile on Main Street?*"

Before the deejay could announce the phone number to call and that hour's prize, which I think was a morning zoo mug, T-shirt, and $100 gift certificate for some local eatery, I casually said, "Jimmy Miller. And, he also produced *Goat's Head Soup*."

After a commercial break, the deejay announced the correct answer, which was Jimmy Miller, the winner's name, and then added the *Goat's Head Soup* factoid. Bob looked genuinely impressed at me.

"How the hell did you know that?"

"I don't know how my mind works. I can't recall details

from yesterday, yet I retain lots of worthless trivia. I just wish I could figure out how to make money with it."

"Well, we'd have been $100 richer, if we had called in." Bob thought for a moment, "So dazzle me! What other trivia do you know?"

"It doesn't work that way. I can't just recite facts and figures; you need to ask me something specific. The question will trigger my memory for the answer."

"C'mon," Bob pleaded. "Share something fun that I don't know."

"All right, let me think a minute." After a few moments, I said, "Did you know that in 1980, only nine-point-seven per cent of Americans were cremated? Last year, close to double that, almost 20%, were cremated." I paused for a moment and then smiled, "It's the *hot* new trend. Pun intended!" Apparently, the morning zoo show was starting to corrupt me.

Bob grinned at my lame joke. "Okay, that's good; *hot* new trend." Looking perplexed, he asked, "Why would you know that?"

"I've been collecting weird trivia since I began my *To Die For* photography shows."

Since 1992, I had been exhibiting cemetery and celebrity gravestone photography at local Chicago galleries and coffee shops as a creative outlet. My exhibits were called, *To Die For: A Celebration of Cemeteries and the Lighter Side of Death*, and included images from my "Graves of the Rich'n'Famous" collection, that showcased the gravesites of Edgar Allen Poe, Jim Morrison, Jimi Hendrix, Karl Marx, Marilyn Monroe and James Dean, among others. Although the subject matter could be construed as being morbid, or perhaps depressing, I stressed a "seize the day" message to viewers: Life is fleeting, so live each day to its fullest. And since death is inevitable, I figured why not scrutinize it, find humor within it, and thus neutralize its frightful, anxiety-producing grasp. As Woody Allen once said, "I'm not afraid of death; I just don't want to be there when it happens."

"I think I might pull together a book of images along with

fun, offbeat trivia. Y'know, put the 'fun' back into funeral."

"If that's your dream, my son, pursue it. *Zie mir gezunt.*"

I looked at him quizzically.

"That's Yiddish for 'be well', as in go forth and be well."

"Oh, okay," I nodded. Bob's use of Yiddish was intriguing for me to hear, however I continued to struggle to understand all of the phrases. "Oh, I have one more stat for you," I paused for effect. "Did you know that 95% of all statistics are made up?"

Bob forced a smile. "You're a fun-ny guy, Michael Nay-man. But let's leave the humor to the professionals," he said, alluding to the radio deejays. He had emphasized each syllable and rolled his eyes at my lame attempt at humor. One thing I appreciated about Bob was his attention to pronouncing my last name correctly, something that people rarely did. My last name only contained six letters, yet the silent "j" tripped up most everyone. In fact, I never made an attempt to correct anyone because it happened so often. I had been referred to as Nee-jam, Nay-jam, Nee-men, and other configurations, but rarely Nay-man, the proper pronunciation.

Lighter moments with Bob were nice, especially since his go-go-go attitude was starting to take its toll on me. Worst of all, he was not open to even discussing Boulder or going to Rocky Mountain National Park. Apparently, we were on a direct route to Palm Springs with no stopovers for capturing keepsake Kodak Moments. However, that was not our agreement. We were supposed to stop along the way, enjoy the sights, and take a few pictures. Again I thought about making it an issue, but decided to hold off until it became more of a concern.

Our previous travel days were filled with flat, boring countryside, but now we were in the mountains. Bob was driving, which gave me ample time to look out the window at the glorious scenery. The road became more winding and steep. Since our vehicle was regulated to 55 mph, we stayed in the far right lane of the four-lane road, nearest the guardrail (when there was one) and a steep drop. As a control freak, my inability to brake was stressing me out and Bob drove as if he really trusted the brakes. In my mind, a rented truck was hardly the epitome of mechanical dependability or safety. Was regular maintenance was conducted on our vehicle? Was the mechanic mindful of doing a good job? For all I knew, the rental company had cut costs to increase their profit margin, or the mechanic hated his job and did a half-ass effort to maintain the vehicle. What did he care? It wasn't his truck!

Going uphill was not too bad, but driving downhill was fucking frightening! I imagined the brakes burning out and our uncontrollable departure from the mountain and down the steep ravine. As we flew down a particularly steep and winding road, all I could do was press down hard on an imaginary brake on the passenger side, close my eyes, and hold my breath. I tried my best to internalize my fear, but at one point as we picked up a great deal of speed going down a steep incline, I blurted out a concerned, "Watch it, Bob!"

Bob immediately became hyper-alert and thought there was someone on the road that he didn't see, and braked hard. "What? What? What's wrong?"

"You didn't need to jam on the brakes, I just wanted you to slow down a bit."

"You asshole, you could have gotten us killed," Bob barked at me. "You scared the shit out of me."

"I'm sorry. This mountain driving is making me nervous. I didn't mean to scare you."

"Do me a favor," he said in a very calm and soft voice, as if he were speaking to a very young child. "As the passenger, you really need to not judge my driving and, above all, do not yell at me to slow down or brake." He took a deep breath and continued, "You may really, really feel a need to say something, but fight it. Don't say a word. And, I'll do the same with you when you drive. Trust me. We'll all be happier. SHUT. UP. PLEASE!"

He was right, but I didn't appreciate the patriarchal patronizing tone and the condescending attitude. He was not my father, and I didn't need a surrogate on this trip. I opened my journal, trying to keep occupied, and jotted down a few observations in silence. As I thought about it, looking down and focusing on my writing was actually a good technique for keeping my eyes off the road. What I didn't see wouldn't scare me.

After leaving Golden, we drove almost 90 minutes to Vail, where we stopped for coffee at the Jitters'n'Shakes Café. At this point, I felt like ordering a *Café Mocha Vodka Valium Latte*. It would have certainly helped to take the edge off, but in reality, I needed a cappuccino with at least six shots of espresso to keep me alert on the road. We took our coffee "to go" and I placed a dollar in their "Thanks a latte" tips jar.

It was now my turn to drive, so I got behind the wheel and drove us back to the road. Just outside of Vail we noticed a sign for a town called, No Name, Colorado.

"What the hell! What did they do? Give up because they ran out of descriptions for their town? That's just downright lazy! It makes those Carlock, Illinois people seem like over-achievers!" I looked over to Bob who had a list scribbled on a small piece of paper tucked into the road atlas.

"I'm creating a Top Ten list of bizarre, offbeat town names," he said, apparently my fascination with lists had inspired him to make one of his own. "So far I have: Hell, Michigan; Disappointment, Kentucky; Truth or Consequences, New Mexico; French Lick, Indiana; and No Name, Colorado." After a brief pause he added, "In no particular order."

"What about Boring, Oregon?"

"That wasn't a confirmed name. I'd better check that out." He flipped the atlas pages until he found Oregon and started his search. As he looked, I noted the fluctuating weather conditions on our drive as we made our way through the mountains. We went from snow to sun, to snow again, within a matter of moments.

"Found it," Bob said triumphantly. "It's located just southeast of Portland,." He pointed to a location on the map.

The radio had brought good news when it became apparent

that we were losing the morning zoo station as the airwaves began to fill with static, and fragments of other stations bled through. I turned the dial slightly and "You Light Up My Life," a syrupy pop song I never ever, ever needed to hear again, filled the truck cabin. After another few turns of the tuning knob, I'd heard one undesirable station after another. It became a very futile and frustrating effort.

"Let's give the radio a rest, I guess," I said, thinking of how wonderful it would be if we could actually play one of the several cassettes I had in my bag. I knew stretches of shitty radio were inevitable on the road, and had my tapes for just such a musical emergency. Had Bob only arranged to have a freaking cassette player in the vehicle, we could be listening to Tom Petty right now, this very instant! *Idiot*, I thought. *Moron!* A simple detail that he totally botched and now, I had to suffer for his inept attention to detail. I looked over at him and he was staring out the window. If he only knew how upset I was at that moment.

Signs alongside the road indicated that we were less than three hours from the Utah state line, so I started to think ahead.

"Hey, Bob," I began. "We should be over the Utah state line in about three hours or so.

"Yeah, I figure it'll be about 30 minutes outside of Grand Junction."

"Right," I continued, "just the other side of the state line is Arches National Park, and it's not too far off of 70. I'd really like to stop and check it out. It's supposed to be really beautiful."

"What is that, one of your *musts?"* he said with more than a hint of sarcasm.

"Actually, yes it is," was my forthright reply.

"We'll see. I dunno. It's just a bunch of rocks, isn't it?"

Jerk! I couldn't understand how a guy who was so creative and sensitive when it came to art, could have so very little appreciation for nature and its inherent beauty.

"I guess you could say that. But then you could say that the

Grand Canyon is just a big hole in the ground," I said, seething with sarcasm.

"My point exactly," he responded calmly.

That's it! I'm pissed!

"Bob, one of the reasons I agreed to this trip was because you gave me the distinct impression that we'd be stopping along the way to enjoy the sights."

"What? McDonald's and Holiday Inns aren't enough?" he teased playfully.

"C'mon, I'm serious here," I whined, not appreciating his flippant attitude. He had lied and I was fed up, I needed to remain calm.

"I'd really like to hike around a bit, take a few pictures, and savor a few Kodak Moments beyond images of parking lots and exit signs."

"Okay, okay," he said, no doubt in an effort to silence me. "Let's stop someplace in Grand Junction for lunch and we can look at your Arches on the map. With any luck, they're near the interstate."

Success, I thought. Finally, I can really start enjoying the road trip by experiencing some scenery beyond what we were seeing from the highway. I smiled and took a deep breath. Life was good, at least for the moment.

Unfortunately for me, moments are brief, fleeting experiences.

As we drove down the road in silence, my eyes fixed on a point several miles ahead, my mind clicked on autopilot and my thoughts began to drift. I started to analyze our discussion about Jennifer from the previous day and decided it was worth re-visiting. Perhaps I should have kept my thoughts to myself; however, as a true extrovert, I needed to verbalize my concerns out loud and obviously within earshot of Bob, my road-weary Confessor.

"You know I was thinking about what set off the whole chain of events. Y'know, Jennifer asking me to move out."

"Really?" Bob mildly began his protest. "You want to go there again?

I sensed that he was appreciating the quiet, and he probably wanted to avoid a conversation that could escalate into another argument.

"Just briefly," I assured him. "I'm still sorting this stuff out and it would be really helpful for me to process this a bit more with you."

Bob looked down his nose and over his glasses at me and smiled. He knew he was trapped. I seized the moment.

"I was reading an article in *Psychology Today*, about ending relationships and moving on. The title was something like, I dunno, 'Moving On and Not Feeling Guilty,' or something like that. And, when she asked me what I was reading, I said, 'Moving OUT and Not Feeling Guilty.' We both caught my Freudian Slip. I tried to back-peddle, but it was out there. So, she got really upset."

"Of course!" Bob returned to his role as my truck-driving therapist. "Didn't you tell me her dad died when she was a teenager?"

I nodded.

"She had abandonment issues to begin with, and you told her you're going to abandon her."

Good point, I thought.

"Y'know I never realized that until now," I admitted as I started to connect the dots. "It got worse though. Then her best friend, whom Jennifer adored, found out that she had cancer and that she most likely wouldn't survive. The girlfriend asked Jennifer to tell her two boys because she had such a good rapport with them."

"Really? Yow, I wouldn't know what to say," Bob said as he continued his analysis. "So, Jennifer now had to deal with the abandonment issue with you, as well as reliving the death of her father through her best friend's situation."

Bob shook his head, "And talk about stress. Not only did she have to deal with another potential loss, but she was given the role of having to tell her friend's sons."

I nodded in agreement.

"So, she made it clear to me that she wanted to deal with this stuff alone. Besides, I was being a shitty partner at this point and of no help as she tried to cope."

"She said you were a shitty partner?"

"No, that was my personal assessment," I admitted. "I gotta be honest with myself here. I was self-centered and only concerned about how these events affected me. I guess I didn't realize how bad things were for her."

Bob nodded in agreement with my conclusion. I felt very badly about the situation, worse than before, and wished I could share my newfound wisdom with her and apologize. I knew that train had left the station, but I wondered if I could intercept it further down the tracks.

"So, I moved out in the fall so we would have our space to think things through," I continued. "In the back of my mind though, I assumed we would work everything out. But come January, I panicked because we were no longer communicating about *us*. We just talked about our individual needs. There was no *us* anymore. Not good, right?"

"At that point, she was truly alone," Bob said. "Absolute abandonment. She needed to realize that she was still a confident person and capable of coping with these issues. She needed to tap into that part of herself."

"You're right. I needed to be there for her, and instead I was into my own shit, my own needs." I paused for a moment as I processed this new information. "Thanks, Bob. We put together these pieces in a few hours; something I was unable to do during months of therapy with Pierre."

"Only you could find a therapist named Pierre," Bob snickered, although I didn't really know what he meant by that. "Sometimes it's easier for someone who's known you for a long time to give you an outside perspective. You're too close to it to see answers."

"I'm so focused on finding solutions that I wrote in my journal before we left that the goal of the trip was to determine what I want and pursue it. That making no decision is the wrong decision. I really need to stop idling in neutral. It's exhausting. I wouldn't commit to Jennifer. I kept trying to keep our relationship from progressing."

"Y'know, something else just occurred to me," Bob said as his face lit up. I could practically see the light bulb beaming above his head. "Jennifer didn't have a good relationship with her father, right?"

"Right. They didn't get along. He was very strict and overbearing. She rebelled. Pretty typical, I guess. But the kicker is that he died suddenly when she was sixteen or so. She never had a chance to work things out with him."

"Okay, and Candy, she didn't get along with her father either, right?"

"That's an understatement. She hated her stepfather. He was abusive and hurtful. And, she didn't know her biological dad. They never met and when she reached out to him, he shut her out."

"So, you have this thing for choosing women who basically hate their fathers. Think about it. They hate the primary male role model in their lives. Then, you come along."

"And, I pay for the sins of the father, more-or-less."

"Exactly," Bob declared with glee, proud of his insight. He looked so very satisfied with his deduction. "It's hard to find happiness with a man when you didn't love or trust your primary male role model."

"Wow, I never thought of it that way." Bob's analysis made sense; the dots were connecting at a rapid rate.

As I thought about it, there were other women I had been involved with that had similar situations. They had poor relationships with their fathers, or they downright hated them. I certainly needed to do a better job of screening potential partners with this problem. No need to have a romantic partner work out her daddy issues with me.

I should have felt some relief, some joy, that thanks to Bob, I now better understood my relationship problems. Instead, I felt more depressed. I started to feel more emotion and a sense of frustration, the start of a downward spiral. Making decisions was hard enough for me, but now I was getting paranoid about my ability to make *good* decisions.

Somewhere along the way I had heard that people fall for the same type of person over and over, drawn to what we know, not what's best. Familiar territory provided comfort. Nevertheless, with this new awareness, I could change my habitual dating preference and find a better choice for me.

My romantic decision-making may have been rocky, but I also felt my career choice was equally dicey. Since Bob was on a hot streak, I shared a professional concern with him.

"I talk about leaving my job to go write, but I never do," I continued, hoping Bob was open to analyzing more than just my love life. I suppose I should have thought of some transition as we shifted topics.

"Instead, I approach writing half-assed. I write when time permits instead of making it a priority."

"You're afraid to commit," Bob interjected without hesitation. It was apparent that he was open to discussing another aspect of my life.

"It's too risky for you," he continued. "You're afraid to leave your job and dedicate your time to writing."

He was right, but it didn't change my main concern. "Well, I'm totally on my own, Bob," I reminded him. "I need a steady paycheck."

"But, you're not giving it a chance."

In a way, he was right. But with Maslow's Hierarchy of Needs, how could I pursue creative endeavors while I'm freaking out about where my next meal is coming from or if I can pay my rent? His comments left me feeling very uneasy and uncomfortable. By not taking risks, was I limiting my happiness?

"It's not unlike your situation with Jennifer," he added after a pause.

"Maybe I didn't commit to Jennifer because she just wasn't right for me," I shared, a belief I had contemplated many times before. "I think I would have known by now. I would have known she was *the one*. Like you knew about Ed. I expect that it should have happened right away."

"It's different for everyone, I guess. It's not fair to think that *love at first sight* is the key to deciding who you should pair off with for the rest of your life," Bob said. Again he paused a moment, I think he was further processing the situation.

"You two probably needed to take some time to discover each other. Maybe some things were good, and others weren't. Were you looking for the ideal, perfect relationship?"

I thought about that for a moment. "Maybe. Well, knowing me, I guess I was expecting the Hollywood rom-com situation where two parties meet, fall in love, and live happily-ever-after. So, I guess, in my mind, we weren't really in love, not unconditionally."

"Well something must have kept you two together for so long."

"The sex was good," I answered quickly with a smile. "At first there was a lot of passion. You know, the newness of a relationship. Then, that faded. I dunno, I really struggle with deciding if someone is *the one*. You know, I always feel like what I have isn't as good as "someone else" out there, some fantasy woman in my mind who's ideal for me. Plus, I guess my confidence in relationships is still shaky after Candy."

"You got divorced in 1982, it's now 1997. Get over it!" Bob barked. He may have been right, but his delivery was harsh.

"All you have to show for your love life the past 15 years is a string of relationships, all void of commitment," he continued. He paused and then got snarky, "I'll bet you're a great date. Interesting. Good looking. You go to a lot of concerts and cultural events. But the bottom line is that you are a shitty partner. You don't seem to like the woman you're with. In fact, I don't think you like women at all," he declared with his usual blunt way. No filter. No sugarcoating.

"I *love* women!" I protested. I wasn't evil. I was a good person.

"No you don't," Bob insisted, his tone becoming more direct and condemning as he continued. "If you did, you'd commit to one of them rather than stringing them along and ultimately dumping them!"

"Fuck you!" Once again I relied on an angry, ignorant outburst of a response. Once again, he had pushed a button, insulting me. And once again, Bob had called me on my bullshit, which was really upsetting to me. It may not have been what I wanted to hear, but it was what I *needed* to hear. At the time, though, I didn't realize that. At that moment, I wanted to pull over, stop the vehicle, and find a way home. I was experiencing the *fight or flight* response, and running away was my preference. I didn't want to be with him anymore. I didn't want to be with anyone anymore. I wanted to be alone, alone to think.

"No, fuck me!" I said hitting myself in the thigh with my fist. Bob looked startled by my aggression. I felt stupid and inept. *How could I keep making the same mistakes over and over? What was wrong with me?*

Not only was I upset with myself, I was also angry about Bob's delivery of the news. My style was always to lather a man before I shaved him. Bob was direct. He made no effort to make his commentary any more pleasant or appealing to me.

I had to remind myself that he was not my mommy; he wasn't required to be gentle with his feedback. He was just the messenger.

Besides, I had been the one who wanted to discuss my issues with him. I should have prepared myself for his unwavering outspokenness, and feared the worst from the beginning. Of course the answers he provided were those I didn't want to hear, because they were accurate, truthful and required change.

I needed time to think. I had just become conscience of the mistakes I had been making. There was newfound clarity. Unfortunately for me, I didn't like what I was learning about myself. I was a screw-up, a loser. Perhaps I was a leopard with spots that couldn't be changed. The very thought made me sad. I was mad at Bob, I was mad at myself; hell, I was just *mad!*

Our rolling confessional was quiet for what seemed like hours, although only a matter of minutes had passed. A sign for several eateries came into view for the upcoming Grand Junction exit and it was time for our road trip therapy session to come to a close, at least for now. Somehow I knew that our discussions were going to be helpful to me as I sought a way to better understand myself and change who I was, but I wondered if my redemption would soon cost us our friendship.

Chapter 14

Seeking Solace with Ho Hos

At Grand Junction, we gassed up and grabbed a sandwich at a Subway. I wasn't very talkative at first, but I made a somewhat lame attempt to lighten the mood a bit.

"Sorry about my outburst," I began as we sat down to enjoy our meal.

"Colorful choice of words back there."

Doing my best professorial imitation, I said, "It was quite the mental exercise to select just the perfect words to capture the moment. I'm not sure I chose well. Perhaps I was a bit hasty with my efforts as a wordsmith."

"I don't know," Bob played along. "'Screw you' wouldn't have been as powerful. No, I think you were successful." He smiled. I knew that we were okay.

After lunch, Bob volunteered to get behind the wheel, and I didn't bother to argue, as I wanted an opportunity to jot down a few notes in my journal and contemplate our last discussion.

Within 30 minutes, we passed the state line into Utah, and the terrain around us seemed to change dramatically, as if we had crossed into Mars. There were colorful rock formations that looked as if they had bubbled up from the innermost depths of the earth and hardened in place, rounded by the wind and baked dry by the sun. The land looked supernatural, like a Roger Dean graphic for a Yes album.

We also observed fewer cars and more and more pick-up trucks with handy gun racks installed behind the drivers' heads.

"Keep your friends close, and your guns closer," I gulped. For the first time on our trip, we both felt out-of-place and all alone. I said a silent prayer for our truck to remain moving and not break down.

"I can see the headline now, 'Gay Jewish artist, and friend, found beaten to death on roadside,'" Bob half-joked.

"Trust me, if we get beaten to death, no one will find the bodies out here," I smiled uneasily.

The combination of having a fairly large lunch, the heat of the day, and the hypnotic, calming effect of rolling down the road lulled me to nod out and sleep a bit.

As my eyes opened, we were pulling into a truck stop.

Trying to make sense of where we were, I asked, "What's going on? Where are we?" Several signs around the truck stop gave me our location: Green River, Utah.

"We're making a quick stop. I'm really thirsty and need to use the john," Bob said as we pulled into a parking spot near the building. Something cold to drink sounded really good to me, so I followed along.

Inside the truck stop, a small television by the counter was turned on for basketball as the Chicago Bulls were playing the Miami Heat in the Eastern Conference Finals. The score was tied, but Chicago was up three games to zero for the series. Another win would give them the title. I loved the Bulls and had partied in the streets when they won 1992 and 1993 championships. At the time, I was living in Wrigleyville with Jennifer and we danced and screamed up and down North Clark Street. Ironically, we were celebrating in the shadows of Wrigley Field, the home of the beleaguered Chicago Cubs who hadn't won a world series since 1908, the longest drought of any major North American professional sports team. Last year, in 1996, I had watched the Bulls in the playoffs while in the Tokyo airport on my way home from Thailand. That's why even watching a few minutes of the game made me happy: it was a piece of *home*.

"C'mon, let's get going, Patrick," Bob said impatiently, not at all interested in basketball. He called me Patrick sometimes, in reference to how I was often mistaken for the actor Patrick Swayze, a fact that drew attention away from him and toward me. I think that's why he would use it as a subtle dig.

I was standing with a few other people, a young couple and an older man.

"Are you going to use the bathroom or is it not clean enough for you?" Bob teased in a voice loud enough for all to hear. Suddenly, I became the center of attention as I could sense everyone staring at me. Humiliated, I tried to laugh off the comment.

"I'm sure the facilities here are fine. No need just now," I said with a playful smile. "In fact, I'm going to grab a Coke because I think I'm a bit dehydrated."

I paid for the large bottle of Coca-Cola along with a package of Hostess Ho Hos – one of my all-time favorite guilty pleasures, and a necessity when I wanted to treat myself after a tough day at work. This day would definitely fall into that category even though I wasn't in my office.

As we walked back to the truck, it suddenly occurred to me.

"Hey, wait a minute! We're well past Arches National Park! I thought we were going to stop! It was a must!"

"Enough with the *musts!*" he said, like a very frustrated older Jewish brother. He then responded sheepishly, "You were asleep. I didn't want to wake you. Besides, it was a good 20 miles off of 70. Quite a bit out of our way."

I stopped in my tracks and glared at him. If looks could kill, he would have been instantly incinerated and left as nothing but a pile of ashes on the ground.

Sensing the laser-hot glare from my eyes, Bob turned to me,

"What? It's not a big deal to miss Arches National Park. I'm sure we'll see lots of *Golden Arches* along the way."

He sounded annoyed, like how dare I complain about not stopping to see some stupid rock formation. After 48 hours of four-lane highways, parking lots, and funky hotel rooms, I really needed a calming, life-affirming nature fix.

"What the hell!" I was very upset and no amount of Ho Hos — even a truckload— was going to make me feel better. *What a jerk,* I thought, *and a control freak!* Well, that was about to change. Now, I would be in control.

"Give me the keys, *I'm driving!*" I delivered that line with a maniacal grin reminiscent of Jack Nicholson's The Joker, minus the make-up, from *Batman.*

Bob didn't argue and tossed me the keys. I wolfed down my Ho Hos, licked the chocolate remains from my fingers, and gulped down the residue with some Coke. I was now in charge, I had a mean sugar buzz, and I was going to stop wherever I damn well pleased!

Chapter 15

Taking Matters into My Own Hands

Poetically, The Who's "Won't Get Fooled Again" played on the truck's radio as I got behind the wheel and sped down the road. I defiantly turned it up and sung along especially loud during the refrain. It was impossible for Bob not to get the connection.

For the next thirty minutes unbeknownst to Bob, I ruminated on our friendship and how challenging it had become for me at times. My inner-dialogue began building a case against the defendant as I checked off a growing list of actions and comments that were often humiliating, frustrating or aggravating.

Granted, I was grateful for his insights and observations about me, and I had no one to blame but myself for his feedback as I had invited his comments.

However, his blatant disregard for my needs on the trip and his increasingly condescending tone were really becoming more irritating and provoking as the miles sped by.

Patience was a virtue well outside my grasp. Now, add the

heat, confinement in a claustrophobic space, and limited sleep to the equation, and the result was growing more and more combustible.

I was tired of Bob's ongoing faultfinding mission and his need to pick at my vulnerable emotional scabs. I had shared intimate details about myself with him because I trusted him. As a friend, I wanted his support and understanding, not necessarily what I needed to do to fix the situation. In fact, it had become rather irritating that he had become Mr. Answer Man, with a sure-fire, quick-fix solution to any problem I mentioned, a regular Dr. Laura with balls. But was he the glowing example of having lived the perfect life? *How ironic*, I thought, *that here was a guy who was not the best life partner or artistic success, yet he had the gall to tell me, in the most patronizing way sometimes, how to live and succeed in life*. Right or not, his seemingly helpful advice was now becoming more and more annoying.

About a half hour down the road, I spied a scenic rest stop near the Eagle Canyon/Moore Exit. *Time to see the sights*, I thought. I wanted to take a few photos, stretch my legs, and take a break from driving. I also had a dull headache from the last thirty minutes, so I had hoped a rest stop would help to ease the pain. Signaling, I began to pull off the road.

"We're stopping for a Kodak Moment, if you like it or not. In other words, it's a MUST," I said quickly yet distinctly, without giving a moment for Bob to protest as we drove into the parking lot. I began to look for a space to park.

As I stopped the vehicle and shifted into park, I marveled at the expansive view. From where I sat, I could see a striking overlook of a beautiful red sandstone canyon peppered with dark green brush, off in the distance a blue mountain range. *Yes, this will do nicely*, I thought as I grabbed my disposable camera out of my bag.

"While others are tethered to their desks at work, we are blessed with an opportunity to see nature at its finest." I said to Bob, sounding like a budding Thoreau.

"Okay, Patrick, whatever makes you happy my Polish

heterosexual friend," Bob said without a hint of enthusiasm, as he opened his door to exit. Once again, in his irritating way, he reduced me to a series of stereotypes and poked fun at my resemblance to the actor Patrick Swayze. I took a deep breath and tried to not let it bother me.

There was a bit of a walk to get to the Lookout Point, maybe fifty yards, much of which was down an incline and then over to a series of large, flat, tan sandstone rocks. I took the lead as we approached a well-worn trail. As we walked, I became more and more excited about the moment.

"This is so cool!" I began. "What an amazing piece of scenery! Y'know in a perfect world, I would be a travel writer and photographer and spend my life going from one beautiful exotic location to another."

"Hopefully, with clean rest stop toilets," Bob teased.

"Ha, ha, very funny." I said dryly, wishing he would stop needling me all the time about my bathroom habits. It was getting old. "I think I'd be a good writer. I free-lanced awhile back. The papers published my stuff with minimal editing."

I felt a need to brag a bit to feel better about myself and to help convince him that I had potential, however dragging out an almost ten-year-old accomplishment seemed lame. I had been successful, but failed to build on it. Time was passing, I was getting older. *Was my fear getting the best of me?*

"If you want to write, then leave your job and write!"

"It's not that easy. I have bills to pay, and I get a decent salary and great benefits. Medical. Dental. Two weeks paid vacation, ten days off for the winter holiday break, and best of all, Fridays off in the summer. Not to mention, working with wonderful people who are like family. That's hard to give up."

"Blah, blah, blah! You're amazing. You can justify anything, if you want," he said snidely.

"What?" I stopped in my tracks, turned and glared into his eyes.

"You dream about writing full-time," he practically shouted at me. "You've talked about it as long as I've known you. Yet you don't do anything about it. You're just afraid to take a risk, afraid to put yourself on the line. You need to stop whining and just do it already! As my grandfather use to say, 'Shit, or get off the pot!' "

Deep down, I knew he was right. But I *was* afraid. I was afraid that I couldn't make enough money as a writer. I was afraid of failure. I was afraid of not being capable of achieving my dream. I didn't respond to him. I just turned around and continued to follow the trail.

My silence seemed to fuel his growing frustration with me. I could hear him take a very deep breath before he continued his rant.

"Writing," Bob scoffed. I couldn't see his face, but I could practically hear his eyes rolling and head shaking. "I can't think of a more impotent act."

He paused for dramatic effect, allowing his words to saturate the air.

"Nobody reads any more," he said with the conviction of an older brother cruelly setting his younger sibling straight on the existence of the Tooth Fairy. He was still walking slightly behind me as we carefully navigated the canyon edge along the trail.

Fair enough, I thought. Not the greatest last words to breathe before leaving this world, but better than some. His remarks sounded much like the faultfinding voice that often resided in my head, critiquing my every goal and dream. My first impulse, admittedly a hasty one, was to push him over the nearby ledge and into the canyon, an immediate solution that would promptly end his antagonistic commentary and thus soothe my throbbing headache. But there were laws about such actions in Utah and I needed to take a deep breath and pause before I did something foolish. For now, such an action would need to remain a fantasy, a daydream designed to help me cope with Mr. Sunshine.

Focus on the natural beauty before me, I thought. I looked out over the canyon and admired the constantly changing red and orange hues of the rocks as shadows from clouds flowed over them, providing a kinetic light show.

Soak in the grandeur of nature, block out Bob's nasal negativity. *Soak in nature, block out negativity*, I silently chanted.

The throbbing pain in my head began to subside and my breathing shifted from tight, shallow breaths to those more deep and cleansing. I was in the moment, fully enjoying the setting and my opportunity to appreciate this incredible view. I stared at the canyon with great intensity, burning the image into my memory so that I could retrieve it for future enjoyment during those bland, dreary days to come when I'd be tethered to my desk back in my office. *Life is good*, the voice in my mind declared, *and I am a lucky man to experience this moment*.

"When can we fucking leave?" Bob said abruptly with a deep nasal whine, invading my Zen moment like an 8.3 magnitude earthquake.

My next move was spontaneous and fluid, emotional and angry. I grabbed Bob by the collar of his shirt, crushing fabric within my tight grasp, and then pushed him just beyond the trail's edge. His toes were on terra firma, while his heels were unsupported by the ground. Only my ten fingers clenching his collar were keeping him from plunging more than 300-feet over the cliff. We were face-to-face, so I could see the panic in his eyes.

"I'm going to throw you into the motherfucking canyon!" I declared, apparently with considerable volume as I sensed many of the tourists around us stopping their conversations and photo-taking to observe Bob's predicament.

The canyon's updraft provided a slight breeze that tickled the hair on my legs and then traveled up into my hiking shorts. This sensation caused me to pause, take a very deep breath, and contemplate my next move.

For the first time all day, he was silent.

Today was Day Three of a road trip with an expiration date that had maxed out 24 hours earlier; a road trip that just ten days earlier had seemed like an excellent chance to have some fun with my buddy while sorting out a few personal problems. But now it appeared that our westward excursion had taken a wrong turn and we were on one heck of a rocky road, and heading for this cliff. I had grown tired of his steady stream of teasing, sarcasm, and sense of superiority. Not that he wasn't right most of the time, but that just made his commentary all the more unbearable to hear. Hell, I realized I was often in denial, but an honest assessment of my particular situation wasn't necessarily what I wanted to hear. I just wanted a supportive reaction from a friend. I was confused as I dealt with my emotions, and although his insights were helping me sort it all out, I still harbored a lot of frustration and anxiety, which added to my tension.

After a nearly 15-year friendship, I thought that I knew him; however, it became painfully obvious that this wasn't the case. He had a secret life that he hadn't shared with me until recently. As a result, I felt betrayed, lied to, and marginalized. Didn't he trust that I would have supported him no matter what? Who was I to judge? I had an open mind and, most importantly, I was his friend.

Writing is an impotent act, the gist of his words shrewdly designed to undermine my desire and confidence to become a writer, was the spark that ignited my growing frustration and anxiety. My explosive reaction was the result of his on-going nagging, impatience and self-centered need to get back into the vehicle and quickly on to our destination, stopping only for physiological needs such as restrooms, repose, and life-supporting nourishment, but nothing more. Bob's insensitive comment, combined with his whiny, childish antics from earlier in the day, had driven me to this explosive breaking point.

Like best friends and siblings often do, he had exploited my weaknesses and playfully harassed me in a constant and twisted game of getting a rise out of me. Hardly a shocking development, but this time, he had sorely underestimated my tolerance for his boorish behavior. This time, he had gone too far. I needed to stand up to him, confront his bullying and declare my boundaries for such antics.

"You lied to me!" I said, gritting my teeth. The sun made me squint, so he couldn't see the rage in my eyes.

Bob looked at me and then down at my fists clenching his shirt, a rush of adrenaline causing my hands to shake slightly. Then, he looked to the side and over his shoulder at the floor of the canyon, a fatal drop below.

Bob saw his future. And he gulped.

Chapter 16

Where Happiness is a Warm Gun

"I didn't lie to you," he said, his eyes reflecting the fear of my sudden angry outburst. I was breathing so hard that I was nearly hyperventilating. He continued with a stammer, "At-at least not intentionally. I wanted us to take our time and travel across the country, but now – now, I just want to get home to *Edward. I miss my home."*

I paused, let his words sink in and exhaled slowly. I didn't argue. He had a partner and a place to be. I didn't.

I suddenly felt lost and alone, like a dog after a rainstorm, trying to pick up a scent to get back home, but it had all been washed away. I pulled Bob toward me, onto solid ground, and let go of his shirt. Embarrassed, I looked down and turned around away from the cliff's edge, softly saying I was sorry, as we slowly walked back to the truck. The show was over and the group of tourists paying attention went back to their business of taking pictures and enjoying the view.

The voice in my head was in full attack mode as it denigrated me without mercy. *What a ridiculous outburst! What are you, ten? You are not an adult, you idiot! Why do you let him get to you? Don't you ever learn? Loser! Loser! Loser!*

The bottom line was that no one ever needed to be critical of me, as I held the title for beating myself up all on my own.

As I managed to silence the voice, I could clearly see that Bob had what I wanted most in life, more than writing full-time or traveling around the world. Bob was in a committed relationship with someone who loved him unconditionally. In my mind, that was The Brass Ring, life's greatest prize, and I was jealous that it was out of my reach at the moment. I fully understood his desire to get back home to Edward, and to do so directly. However, I could also see that he needed to uphold his part of the bargain and stop at a few points of interest along the way, as he had promised. As a friend, Bob was not being fair or considerate. His needs were not the only priority, I also had needs!

Slowly, my breathing became more relaxed and I began to realize that my anger wasn't just with Bob and his behavior, I was angry with *me*. I was angry about the mistakes I was making with my romantic relationships, mistakes I kept repeating. I was a bright, caring, interesting person, yet I was alone. *Why hadn't I recognized my errors sooner?*

"Maybe I should drive," Bob offered in a calm, soothing tone, and I accepted his offer with a nod.

For now, I just wanted to sit quietly and sort out what just happened. Sure, Bob's behavior was rude and his comments disparaging, but it didn't merit me throwing him off a cliff. Truth be told, my intention was not to injure Bob, but merely to threaten him. I sought to scare him enough so that he knew he had crossed the line and he needed to respect that line in the future. Some of my anger was for show, play-acting. Sure, he pissed me off, but just telling him off, or calling him a "jerk" or "asshole," wouldn't have changed his behavior. I knew Bob, and I knew I needed to add a little drama to the situation to get what I needed for me.

"Hey, what happened back there," Bob began, again in a calm soothing tone. "I don't know when to stop sometimes.

I've been pushing us pretty hard and I know you want to stop from time to time to enjoy nature. I get it. I'll be better about that."

He seemed genuinely concerned, and sorry, even though he didn't outright apologize.

YES! The voice in my head was now in celebration mode. *SUCCESS!* Inside there was a full marching band playing and confetti raining down as I danced around, while on the outside, I managed to remain somber.

"Me too," I said softly. "I'll try to keep my temper in check." He didn't see me smile slightly as my gaze returned to the scenery outside my passenger window. On days like this, even small successes had to be embraced and celebrated.

As we drove along, I observed that the dynamic Utah landscape provided a welcomed diversion – a detour – from the emotions of the day. Parts of the state with its colored, layered rocks, looked like the Badlands of South Dakota, but on steroids! The rocks were beautiful as they changed hue with the movement of the sun and clouds, and were mesmerizing to watch. Yet they were also desolate and uninviting.

There were long stretches of road on Route 70 without any services, or any traffic for that matter. For mile upon tedious mile, we didn't see any sign of another human being or even an animal or bird, not even road kill; just an occasional road sign. The skies were devoid of ubiquitous jet traffic. We felt very isolated and alone. It had been hours since we had seen another vehicle, and to the best of my memory, we hadn't seen anyone since the Eagle Canyon Rest Area. If we had traveled in the darkness of night, I would have certainly scanned the skies for space ships and aliens.

We soon turned south on to Route 15, the road that would take us the last leg of the trip to San Bernardino, where we would exit on to Route 10 east to Palm Springs. Depending on how long and hard we drove, I calculated that we could make it to Palm Springs sometime in the afternoon the following day.

The absence of fast food signs led to a craving for something to eat: One definitely wants what one can't have, and we were both getting really hungry.

"I don't know about you, but I could use a Quarter Pounder with cheese," I said, wishing I had kept a stash of candy bars or trail mix in my duffel bag. Even though I knew I'd come up empty, I began looking for anything edible in my bag. Surely, there'd be a pack of gum, or some morsel of food I had forgotten about. I looked everywhere, in every pocket, but nothing was to be found. All I had was a plastic bottle of warm water with only a few sips left.

"I keep telling myself that we'll stop at the next exit with services, but there isn't," Bob said with a hint of frustration.

I kept scanning the horizon for any road sign promising an upcoming restaurant, or at the bare minimum a rest stop with vending machines. But, there was nothing!

Then, off in the distance, I spied what looked like a McDonalds sign, near the road. *Was it a mirage?* I thought.

"Hey, is that what I think it is?" I shouted, like a shipmate in the crow's nest.

Bob strained to see the approaching red and yellow dot on the horizon, then confirmed my assessment. "Quarter pounders, here we come!"

We were driving as fast as our truck would allow, but it seemed like it took ages to clearly see the restaurant and a surprisingly full parking lot. My mouth began to water with anticipation.

As we pulled in the parking lot, I noticed that there were no regular cars, only pick-up trucks; more specifically, pick-up trucks with gun racks! What I couldn't fathom though, was where did they come from? We didn't witness any traffic coming or going down the road. They all must have been from parts west I surmised, or they had arrived at this destination from driving across the desert on unpaved trails. But it didn't matter. We were famished and hot, juicy burgers were just steps away. Bob pulled the truck into a space and we got out to stretch our legs and fill our stomachs.

I opened the restaurant door to the din of satisfied customers eating their meals and conversing quite loudly. Bob had barely stepped through the threshold when the conversations all abruptly came to an end, as if someone had pressed the mute button on a magic remote control device. Everyone's eyes focused on us. We tried to be nonchalant as we walked to the counter, but the unwanted attention was unnerving. Why were they staring? Why were we the center of attention? And more importantly, why didn't we use the drive-up window?

Then it occurred to me as I looked at Bob. I had gotten sloppy and let my guard down as his "try-to-fit-into-middle-America" fashion consultant. Today, not only had I allowed him his purple bunny shorts and tight American flag tank top, but he had also adorned himself with a few costume jewelry bracelets and a red purse on his shoulder. I had totally neglected my role as the Traveling Fashion Police. As a result, we had literally stopped conversations as the entire place watched us saunter up to the counter to order. I could only imagine that, in their eyes, we weren't just two guys; we were an openly gay couple. And from what I could ascertain, a rare occurrence in these parts. In my mind, the opening notes of "Dueling Banjos" from *Deliverance* began to play. My greatest fear had come to life! *Was I about to squeal like a pig?*

"So much for going full-stealth," I whispered to Bob.

"Make our order to go, right?" he whispered back.

"Definitely, to go."

We quickly placed our order of food with the blonde-haired, blue-eyed teenage boy behind the counter, and prayed that service was lightning fast so we could return to our vehicle within a blink of an eye and get back on the road.

Uncomfortably, I glanced at the patrons, smiled and nodded. No diversity at all, I thought. In fact, this McDonald's only served vanilla soft-serve ice cream. No chocolate! Or, heaven forbid, *mixed.*

We grabbed our bag of burgers tucked inside a cardboard carrier for our two large drinks, before it even hit the counter, and left as quickly as possible. We flew through the exit doors and out on to the asphalt of the parking lot.

"Feet don't fail me now!" I joked as we bolted back to the truck. Without even fastening our seat belts, Bob turned on the ignition and slammed the transmission into reverse. He pushed the stick shift on the steering column into drive and stomped on the gas pedal, spraying some of the loose gravel on the black top in all directions.

"Go! Go! Go!," I encouraged Bob.

As we pulled on to the road, we couldn't help but notice a window filled with prying eyes still focused on us as we sped away.

"Oh my gawd, what the fuck was that about?" I placed my hand on my chest and took in a deep breath.

"No shit!" Bob said incredulously, with an edge of fear and terror in his voice.

"And I was guilty by association," I laughed nervously, "I can see Utah will not be a vacation destination for gays anytime soon."

With the restaurant in our rear view mirror, we enjoyed our food in the speeding truck, each bite tasting mighty fine as we were grateful to be unscathed and back on the road. It would still be a few more hours before we stopped at our final destination for the day, Cedar City. With limited radio reception, we found ourselves singing Beatles tunes a cappella as we tried to keep ourselves entertained and alert. In honor of our recent restaurant experience, we dedicated "Happiness is a Warm Gun" from the White Album to our gun-toting friends in pick-up trucks.

Chapter 17

Go Thunderbirds!

As we pulled into Cedar City, we quickly assessed our hotel options and decided against the (Not So) Quality Inn and for the Comfort Inn, which was advertising "free HBO" and located just across the street from a well-lit diner. It was half past 6 p.m. according to my watch, and the grumbling of my stomach indicated it was dinnertime.

Bob checked us into the hotel, we dropped off our bags, and went to the diner across the road.

I was exhausted, and after having McDonald's for lunch, I ordered something light and healthy for my meal: a classic Cobb salad and a glass of iced tea. Bob followed my lead and we waited patiently for our order. After an awkward moment, I decided to break the silence.

"What a day, huh? I'm impressed with our stamina, I think we were on the road close to ten hours."

"Yeah, Utah seems to be never-ending. It's just so vast."

"And very well-armed," I quickly added for a laugh.

"Really! I'm just glad we were able to get outta Dodge when

we needed to." Bob joked, imitating Michael Jackson's high-pitched voice, "I'm a *lover* not a *fighter*."

After we finished eating, I thought about excusing myself to go back to the hotel lobby. Zion National Park was coming up and I was curious if there might be a brochure available.

"I'd really like us to stop at Zion tomorrow," I said, exercising my new found confidence after the canyon threat. "It's my last chance to see one of Utah's most famous national parks," I boldly declared, tired of being subtle and ignored.

"Okay," he said with a smile. "Let's do it!"

I couldn't detect if his sudden enthusiasm was really sarcasm, or if he was being genuine. After our moment in Eagle Canyon, I was willing to give him the benefit of the doubt and assume he was supportive of our making a tourist stop at Zion National Park.

"I'm heading back to the hotel lobby to see if there are any brochures on Zion. I'll meet you back at the room."

With that, I left Bob with his after-dinner coffee and walked across the street back to the Comfort Inn.

A very attractive young woman was at the counter, quite a change from the heavy-set, older balding man who checked us in. I assumed he was the manager, and she must be the night shift.

Her nametag read Jodi, and from what I could assess, she looked to be somewhere between her late teens or early twenties. Jodi was busy writing in a spiral notebook and there were three thick, high fashion magazines laid out in front of her, opened to full-page ads showcasing sophisticated models in colorful outfits. As I approached her, she never looked up and seemed to be very deep in thought.

"Hi, I'm sorry to interrupt your work, but I was wondering if you had any brochures on Zion National Park."

Her head bolted up, startled, as if she had suddenly been woken up from a deep sleep.

It took her a moment to focus. "Oh, hi! Zion National Park? Why no we don't. But there's a map over there," she said pointing to a framed map on the wall directly across from the desk. "The park is about an hour southwest of us and you can see that it's very easy to access from Route 15."

I glanced at the map, but it was no different than the one in my road atlas, so it was of little help.

"Have you been there before?" Since I had only Bob to speak with the past three days, it was refreshing to have someone new to converse with. Besides, I wanted to crank up the sleeping Nejman charm, which had been dormant the entire trip.

"Many, many times," she said, practically glowing. "It's a really beautiful place to hike. Is that where you're headed?"

"We're on our way to Palm Springs, but I think my buddy and I will stop and check out the park tomorrow," I said. "I mean it's so close and it'd be a pity not to at least spend an hour or two there."

She looked surprised. "An hour or two? To do it justice you need at least a day or two. Minimum." She smiled and adjusted her dark hair. A few strands were in her face, and she tucked them behind her ear. In my mind, I laughed to myself, *a day or two, not with Bob, ever!*

"I'm sure you're right, but we need to get to Palm Springs soon. My friend is a painter and we have a truckload of his art to get there." I was nervous and sharing too much information. I felt a bit insecure and hoped she'd be impressed with my association with Bob.

"A painter? Really? Would I know his name?

"You might," I said coyly. "*People* magazine called him the 'Windy City Warhol.' We're from Chicago," I added, although that wasn't necessary. I would assume most people know Chicago as the Windy City or the Second City, just like they know Paris as The City of Lights or New York as the Big Apple.

"Obviously," she said, aware of Chicago's nickname. "What's your friend's name?"

"Bob Fischer," I said with assurance, as if I was saying Pablo Picasso or Vincent Van Gogh. She echoed the name and thought for a moment, checking her memory banks to determine if it had a familiar sound or not.

Maybe I was being too informal, I thought. In the art world, he went by Robert A. Fischer. And maybe, I was being too cavalier with the idea that Bob was famous outside of Chicago.

"Well, he's my friend, so I call him Bob, but he's known as Robert A. Fischer. He had a gallery exhibit several months ago in Chicago and we're just transporting his work home."

"If he's the Windy City Warhol, doesn't that mean he's from Chicago?"

Good question, I thought. She was very observant. "Yes, of course. He's from Chicago, but now he lives in Southern California. We're just transferring the last of his work."

Jodi had brown eyes and a sweet smile, very girl-next-door. If I had been a younger man, I would have definitely been flirting with her, however a twenty-year difference between us seemed too vast a chasm to cross. Perhaps, the "old" Michael, the one with unchangeable leopard spots would have made a play for her. But that wasn't who I wanted to be anymore, and if I truly wanted to change, I needed to exhibit the appropriate behavior. I was also out of practice speaking with an attractive woman, so my demeanor was awkward, lacking confidence. In all honesty, I was probably embarrassing myself, but I stumbled on through the effort anyway.

I motioned toward her notebook and the magazines. "Are you writing an article?"

She laughed. "Me? No! This is a project for school. I'm go to SUU and I'm taking a Mass Communications class."

"SUU?"

"Sorry! Southern Utah University," she clarified and then did a quick fist pump into the air like a low-key, bashful cheerleader. "Go Thunderbirds!"

She went on to explain that she was an American Indian and going to school on a scholarship. She was a Communications major, but she wasn't sure what she wanted to be ultimately. The project she was working on had to do with our society and its pursuit of the image of the perfect, ideal woman. Her essay dealt with this unrealistic standard and how it impacts young women's body image, and often leads to eating disorders.

"Women in America strive for this ideal image of what a woman should look like," she explained. "But, it's not at all realistic. The whole Barbie doll look is so unnatural. Large breasts. Tiny waist. Thin, thin, thin. Not to mention the whole Caucasian, blonde-hair, blue-eyed preference. You know, *the* American standard for beauty."

I couldn't help but admire Jodi's dark black hair, brown eyes and brown skin. She was very attractive, but according to our all-American standard of beauty, it was unlikely that she would be gracing the cover of a fashion magazine anytime soon.

"What a strange coincidence, but believe it or not, I used to teach a Mass Com class for a Journalism program back home," I said. "My undergraduate degree was in Journalism, so the class I taught provided an overview of the various media at that time: magazines, newspapers, television and radio.

"I used to challenge my students to seek out and examine magazine covers for various women's magazines and often times, we would discover that the models were 17-year-olds, maybe 18, and air-brushed!"

I continued, "Imagine that: Seventeen-years-old and airbrushed to look thinner or more vibrant. What chance does the average woman have to meet *that* standard?"

"Exactly."

"I used to offer extra credit if my students wrote the editors of the magazine and said they wouldn't buy it in the future if the cover models were not more realistic and at a healthy weight."

"Nice," Jodi said genuinely impressed.

"What's the focus of your paper?" Who was I kidding. I was flirting and doing quite well. It was a harmless exercise to keep my skills honed.

"I've selected three of the top fashion magazines," Jodi pointed to each one. "All are the May issues, and I'm checking to see how many woman of color there are, either on the cover, in articles, or featured in ads."

"And what have you found?" I asked the question, but I already knew the answer.

"A big fat zero! There are no women of color to be found anywhere! In fact, unless you look specifically for a black woman's magazine, like *Essence*, it's nearly impossible to find a black woman on a cover!"

"It's hard to believe that entire groups of women can be ignored!"

Jodi continued, "I don't get it. From a marketing perspective, there are a lot of women of color. A lot! And they certainly have purchasing power. I think it would make commercial sense to expand the standards of beauty to have more diversity!"

Her point was well made, I thought. "Well, it sounds like you have a great thesis for your paper. I'm sure you'll get a great grade!"

She smiled, obviously appreciating my compliment. After an awkward pause, I determined it was best to move along.

"Well good luck with your school work. It's been nice talking with you," I said, smiling and starting to turn away. "Oh, wait!"

A wall near the front desk was dedicated space for sundry items. There were three shelves that were more or less a mini-convenience store. The shelves had simple displays of travel-size versions of toothpaste, aspirin, mouthwash, and other toiletries, as well as a small selection of gum, candy bars, and snacks. Next to the shelves was a small magazine rack with about a dozen options ranging from *Time* to *Good Housekeeping*. A few steps away from the magazine rack was a small refrigerator that contained bottles of various soft drinks and spring water.

"I didn't see this all before," I was pointing to the snacks. "I think I'll pick up a few items."

I grabbed a pre-packaged bag of trail mix, a Snickers bar, and a couple of breakfast bars. The breakfast bars were from a box of six, but they had been subdivided and labeled for individual sale. After today's situation where food was sparse, I wanted snack items to keep on hand. I also grabbed a bottle of water, as I figured it could come in handy as I hiked around Zion. Jodi rang up the items on a small cash register and placed them in a white plastic bag with a yellow smiley face on it, along with a big "Thank You," and I paid her. There was a basket of apples on the counter.

"How much for an apple?"

"No charge for our guests," she said with a smile. So, I grabbed two. "I think my friend might like one, too."

I thanked her and wished her a good night. Our conversation was a really nice way to end a rather stressful day, and it was so very pleasant to hear a woman's voice for a change.

I got back in the room and jotted a quick notation in my journal. I needed to document our progress. I had calculated that we had been on the road about 10 hours, drove approximately 570 miles, made three stops — Green River, Eagle Canyon, McDonalds — and had a potential homicide: Bob's *almost* cliff dive.

Bob was sitting on his bed with HBO on the television. The movie *Clear & Present Danger* was about to start, and it would be a real treat to kick back and watch an action-thriller with Harrison Ford portraying CIA analyst Jack Ryan.

Unfortunately for me, the day had taken its toll: I nodded out about halfway through the movie and fell into a deep sleep.

Chapter 18

Day Four on the road:
Cedar City, Utah to Palm Springs, California

The next morning, I woke up before Bob. I was surprisingly well-rested, relaxed and refreshed. The clock next to my bed indicated that it was almost 7 a.m. With Bob still asleep, I quietly sneaked into the bathroom and closed the door. It was that time again, and I was alone.

Unlike the previous day, my morning constitutional went without a hitch. Life was good. I quickly showered, shaved, brushed my teeth, applied my contact lenses, and dried my hair. Within fifteen minutes, I was ready to start the day except for getting some fresh clothes out of my bag.

As I stepped out of the bathroom, I saw that Bob was all dressed, eating an apple and watching a news show with the sound turned off, an image of President Bill Clinton filled the screen.

"Anything exciting?"

"If my lip-reading skills are accurate, he's saying something about achieving world peace and ending hunger, but I'm skeptical," Bob said dryly.

"As long as there are no nuclear disasters or killer bee infestations, it's a good day," I said as I packed my toiletries back into my bag. "The bathroom's yours. I'm pretty much ready to roll."

Bob finished his apple, tossed the brown-stained core into the wastebasket, and then went to the bathroom, closing the door. I grabbed my favorite T-shirt from my bag, a pale green *Mambo* brand one with a blue orb on it with an attached yellow cross, and got dressed.

"I'm ready for Zion," I proudly proclaimed.

"Let's get going so you can do your hiking thing," Bob said without any prodding from me. "I'll bet there's a place to get breakfast there, so we can hit the road."

We left the Cedar City Comfort Inn at 8 a.m. and headed southwest on Route 15 to Zion National Park. Like a 10-year-old en route to his first trip to Disneyland, I was anxious to get to our destination and begin to explore.

Bob was in the driver's seat and I turned on the radio, hoping for the best. To my pleasant surprise, the driving rhythm and thumping piano of Spirit's "I Got A Line On You" came on and I turned it up, singing along.

I barely got through the refrain when I stopped, realizing how dreadfully out-of-tune I was, a clear reason why I felt more at home *behind* the scenes of music productions and not on stage. Unfortunately for me, I couldn't sing very well or play an instrument, which seemed strange for someone who loved music so very much. I passionately loved music, but I couldn't make any of my own. As the song ended, the deejay came on, briefly gave the time and station's call letters, and then introduced Foghat's "Slow Ride." The musical drought on the airwaves had at last come to an end, at least temporarily, so I sat back and enjoyed it.

To pass the time, I examined the road atlas map of Utah. The area we were in had an abundance of parks and recreational areas. If we weren't on a mission to reunite Bob and Edward, I would certainly want to spend a few days, if not weeks in this part of the country, enjoying Zion National Park, Bryce Canyon National Park, and just 120 miles south in Arizona, The Grand Canyon, which I had been to before, but it would be great to re-visit. For today, I was perfectly happy spending a couple of hours at Zion before we continued our journey through the northwestern tip of Arizona and then on to Nevada and California.

Except for a few short 30-second commercials, our new fave rave radio station provided nearly a solid hour of rock classics including Humble Pie's "30 Days in the Hole," Rick Derringer's "Rock'n'Roll, Hootchie Koo," and Montrose's "Rock Candy." No need for caffeine! This was audio bliss and my arteries were pumping along with the rhythm section of each song. This was music from my youth, a time when I was in high school and spent hours listening to these records while staring at flickering candles, burning incense, and enjoying a slight buzz from the roach I had smoked minutes earlier. Unfortunately for us though, the signal soon faded into a sea of static and we were once again reduced to morning news and Country music.

We followed the road signs to Exit 40 and soon we were at the Zion National Park gate, just outside the Kolob Canyons Visitor Center. I gladly paid the attendant in the booth the $10 entrance fee (good for re-entry for seven days! What a deal!). The receipt he gave us, along with a park map, indicated that it was only 8:56 a.m.! There was plenty of time for me to hike!

Before Bob pulled away from the booth, I asked about the nearest trail.

"Taylor Creek," the attendant said. "About two miles beyond the visitor center."

I thanked him and Bob drove over to the parking lot outside the visitor center.

"Why don't you take the truck? I'm sure there must be somewhere here to get a bite to eat," Bob said as he prepared to leave the vehicle. "Have a good time and I'll wait for you over there." He pointed to a shaded picnic table under a sprawling cottonwood tree.

With that, he took off walking toward the visitor center, and I shifted over to the driver's seat. I put the truck into gear and headed down Kolob Canyons Road about two miles to the Taylor Creek trailhead. I was ecstatic to have my first scheduled *time out* from Bob on the trip. Taylor Creek Trailhead, here I come!

As I pulled into a small parking lot near the trailhead, I realized that Bob hadn't said anything about a time constraint. It seemed that I was free to savor my moment with nature for as long as I needed. The lot was empty, so I pulled into a slot nearest the trail and parked. I grabbed my small backpack — which already contained my disposable camera, a bottle of water and the breakfast treats I secured the night before – and hopped out of the vehicle, throwing the backpack over my right shoulder. After sitting in a truck cab for three days, I was eager to stretch my legs and experience some strenuous physical activity, so I briskly hiked up the trail just short of breaking into a full jog. Just ahead of me was a footbridge that crossed Taylor Creek, and beyond that a deep ravine bordered by tall green Freemont cottonwood trees in the shadows of steep red stone canyon walls.

Crossing the bridge, I took a moment to enjoy the soothing sound of the flowing river as I watched the clear, rather shallow water, rush past the rocks and stones below. Just above the playful rippling sound of the water, I could hear a variety of songbirds as a slight breeze caressed me on its way further down the river. I could see the trail ahead urging me on, so I snapped a few pictures and continued on my way.

The trail's incline began to get steeper and steeper, and my breathing began to get more labored as I climbed higher and higher. Even though I had worked out three times or more a week, no Step Master or treadmill regimen could have prepared me for the strenuous inclined pitch I was racing up, as I eagerly hunted for a place to sit and enjoy the scenic views. After about twenty-five minutes I stopped to enjoy a view of

Taylor Creek far below me, winding further and further into the canyon. The water looked more of a royal blue in contrast to the pale azure of the sky. Snap! Snap! A few more pictures and onward up the trail.

With each step, my heart grew lighter and my smile broader as I soaked in every sight and surrounding sound. Nature was my drug of choice that morning as it seduced my senses and reminded me that there are few joys in life that can match its splendor. I was in a blissful state, far away from my personal problems, isolated from my anxieties for the future, and removed from my regrets of the past.

Fifteen minutes later on the trail, I had reached a perfect place to stop, sit and enjoy an overview of the canyon. To me, it was more appealing to soak in the gorgeous scenery for ten to twenty minutes, rather than go further up the trail with hopes to improve upon the view. Since I had such limited time, I had put my senses on high alert, absorbing all I could, as quickly as possible. I wished I could stop time; freeze it for a while so I could enjoy the canyon at the more leisurely pace of hours rather than minutes.

Using a nearby big, flat rock as a stool, I opened my bag and picnicked on my water and breakfast treats, finishing up all that I had within moments.

Alone on my stone seat, I sat in awe of the beauty in front of me, soaking it all in, and enjoying the moment to the fullest. I blocked out any worries about my age, career goals, lack of a life partner, and especially my travels with Bob. With the sun in my face, sounds of the birds chirping in the background, and the smell of a nearby juniper tree, I prayed with gratitude to God for this incredible moment in time. The steep canyon walls before me were layered in hues of reds, oranges, and browns, as if the Creator had used a massive circular saw to cut into the rock and expose the grain within. All I could think about was how lucky I was to be there to witness this incredible beauty.

The view of the steep canyon walls reminded me of the previous day and the emotionally charged confrontation with

Bob. Deep in thought, I began to assess my situation and how I had gotten to this point in my life. Several of Bob's comments began to penetrate my consciousness. He was right: All I had to show for my love life was a 15-year string of relationships, void of commitment and lacking unconditional acceptance and love. I wasn't the best partner. In fact, I was a pretty *shitty* partner, to use my rather blunt appraisal.

I needed to change. If I didn't, I would be destined to spend my life alone and unhappy. Or at the very least, I'd continue to bounce from one unfulfilling relationship to another, hurting those foolish enough to risk trying to get me to commit.

I needed to become a better person, a better partner, and a better man.

A snap of a twig startled me, ending my meditative state and reminding me that there were others who shared this trail. A young man with a bright yellow Walkman head set worn over his green baseball cap was humming to himself as he strode up the trail. I nodded and smiled.

He stopped, pulling the headphone off his head and brushing his long, curly red hair behind his ears. "Pretty awesome, huh!"

Perfect word choice, I thought. "Yep. Pretty awesome," I conferred. Then, I grabbed my camera and offered it to him. "Hey, would you do me a favor and take my picture? I don't think anyone is going to believe how beautiful this place is."

"Sure!" He put down his Walkman and backpack and I moved into position. I took off my sunglasses and tucked them into the neck of my Mambo t-shirt.

"How's this?" I stepped into the trail, with the sun directly shining on the right side of my face, "Can you get some of the canyon in the background?"

"No problem," he said as he looked through the viewer. "On three. One, two, and three."

With a quick click, the moment was captured and he returned the camera to me.

"Thanks a lot and enjoy your hike," I said.

"Aren't you going any further?" he asked as he collected his Walkman and backpack and started past me.

"Not today, I'm afraid," I said with a hint of sadness. "I'm heading to California and I need to get back on the road."

"Cool!" He said, continuing his economical communication. "Happy trails, dude!"

"Happy trails," I said as he placed the headset back on his head and continued on his way. With a deep sigh, I looked at the canyon one last time and then turned to hike back down the trail. What I lacked in time, I made up with my hyper-awareness of the moment and it was very satisfying. I was truly happy.

Life was good.

Chapter 19

No One to Hear You Scream

I returned to the Kolob Canyons Visitor Center to pick up Bob and found him sitting at the picnic table in the shade, just as we had agreed upon earlier. As soon as I pulled up in the truck, he leapt up and jogged over to me.

"I had oatmeal with raisins!" he said with the glee of a young boy after having indulged in his first banana split with all of the sugary trimmings. "I had a really nice morning people watching, reading the paper and drinking coffee."

A-ha, I thought, *caffeine!* This would explain his considerable energy and enthusiasm.

"So, how was your commune with nature?" Bob opened the passenger side door and hopped into the cab.

A big grin on my lips broke into a toothy smile, "Ah-mazing!"

Bob looked at me, "Good, I'm glad that's over. Let's go!" He paused and stared at me, "My goodness, you're all aglow."

I laughed. "I was so blown away by all the beauty," I said this with much wonder in my voice. I think I was still in awe and struggled to find adequate words to describe my experience. I went on, "The sky. The cliffs. The river…"

"Okay Ansel Adams," he quipped. "Enough already. I get it. No need to elaborate. What's important is that you had your moment with nature, and you're happy. *Mazel tov!*"

I smiled. He was right.

I put the truck into drive and began to pull out of the parking lot. Before we took a left turn to return to the highway, I glanced back from where I had just come.

"You have to admit, it's incredibly beautiful," I said, curious if Bob was capable of feeling the intense pleasure and deep satisfaction I experienced when surrounded by nature at its best.

"Yeah, it's a bunch of rocks and a river," he said frankly. "But I get it."

I raised my eyebrows and nodded. *Makes sense,* I thought. Just because we're best friends doesn't mean we need to enjoy the same things.

As much as I didn't want to leave, I turned on the left turn signal and pulled on to the road and back to the highway. According to my wristwatch, it was just after 10:30 a.m.

"It's funny," I said. "When I was a teenager, all I could talk about was going to Colorado to see mountains. My mom got all upset and started crying. 'Why do you hate us so much? All you ever talk about is getting as far away from us as possible,' " my imitation of her voice was pathetic, but Bob got the idea. "I said, 'I don't hate you guys, I just want to see the world!' "

"So did you get to Colorado?"

"Yep, as soon as I graduated from high school, a buddy and I were going to hitchhike out to Denver together, but he backed out at the last minute. So, I went by myself. Quite the adventure!"

"How was it hitchhiking?"

"Since I was traveling alone, I decided to fly to Denver and hitchhike around the state. I was pretty clueless. My plan was to arrive late and sleep overnight at the Denver airport. I didn't realize it closed down at 10 p.m. So I walked out into the parking lot and put out my thumb. Some guys picked me up and let me sleep on their floor. The next morning they fed me and I went on my way. I had no idea where I was other than somewhere in Denver.

"It was dark when we arrived so I had absolutely no bearings. I walked outside their door and down a flight of stairs, and started down the street. I looked back at the house and there in the background were these unbelievably beautiful purple mountains! I got all choked up. I guess I'm a real sucker for natural beauty," I admitted, waiting for Bob to make some kind of wisecrack, but he didn't.

"So anyway, I hitched a ride from Denver to Colorado Springs, this lady with two kids picked me up in a pick up truck."

"Really?" Bob was genuinely surprised. "A mother with two kids picked you up. You must have either looked angelic or pathetic, like a lost puppy," he quipped.

"I think I must have looked really pathetic with my two-ton backpack and my patched-up jeans. She let me throw my pack in the back of her pick up and I laid back on it for the ride. That pack was way too big and heavy to be practical! I was big into camping, and I wanted to be prepared, so I brought like *everything* on the trip: A two-man tent, down sleeping bag, a small propane tank stove, clothes, an axe and even a heavy grinding stone to keep it sharp. Imagine my taking all that on the plane! I bought the backpack from an old Army surplus store. It had a metal frame that dug into my back, so it was downright painful to use. It was hot and dusty on the road. She must have taken great pity on me. Thank goodness, I got that ride."

"So no one tried to rape or kill you while hitchhiking, huh?"

"No, but I did have a really scary situation," I said. "My next ride was from this old rodeo guy. He used the word 'fuck' at least six times per sentence and I was never sure how to read him. I had long hair and patched jeans. Total hippie. And, he was pretty rough around the edges."

"Cue the 'Dueling Banjos.' "

"No, nothing like that. He asked where I was going and I said Pikes Peak."

"Why Pikes Peak?"

"I dunno, it was the only destination I could think of and I wasn't about to say, 'Wherever you're headed, cowboy.' "

"I'm sure he'd of like to get his brand on you," Bob teased.

"So he said he lived near Pikes Peak, and I'm welcome to stay at this cabin he has on his homestead. I really had no other options, so I said okay. We got to his tiny little cabin, just off the road, with Pikes Peak in the immediate background. Picture perfect! He said that there's a trout stream nearby and a rod and reel in the cabin. Help yourself! See you in the morning. And he took off."

I paused as I pulled our truck back on to the highway and proceeded southwest toward Arizona.

I continued, "It's getting late and the place is literally in the middle of nowhere. Miles from another house or town."

"No one to hear you scream," Bob interjected.

"Right! I started to feel really alone and vulnerable. And hungry. So I figured I would catch a trout for dinner. I grabbed some fishing gear and walked about 20 yards to a stream. As I attached a fly to the line, I noticed this big hairy carcass out of the corner of my eye. I took a closer look and it was this rather large shaggy dog with a big hole in its gut. Someone had shot it!"

"Oh, oh," Bob said, his eyes wide.

"Yep, I am officially creeped out at this point. So I headed back to the cabin to see what food I could scrounge up. All over the cabin there were all these weird medical instruments, big metal syringe-like devices and lots of knives and sheers. Stuff for the cattle, I guessed. But it was all very scary and ominous. And, it was starting to get dark out."

"Really?"

"Uh-huh. I was thinking he was going to come back in the middle of the night, drug me, and rape or kill, or something. I was totally freaked out."

"Then what?"

"I didn't find any food, just a few odds and ends like Crisco oil and some flour, nothing to make a meal out of. Luckily, I had a couple of candy bars in my backpack which was dinner. There was an old potbelly stove, so I made a fire because it started to get pretty chilly once the sun went down.

"It was really dark outside except for a lonely streetlight at the gate at the end of the driveway. No traffic. No sounds except the wind blowing through the cabin."

"No cable TV, huh?" Bob joked.

I laughed, "No, not even basic! Hell, I'd have been happy to watch *U.S. Farm Report* just to hear another voice."

"So, I tried to get comfortable on this little couch. I used my sleeping bag like a blanket and tried to get some sleep, but anytime I heard any little noise at all, I bolted up to check it out. I think I slept with one eye opened the entire night."

"No late night visitors?"

"No, but at sunrise, I looked out the window and saw a red pick-up truck at the end of the driveway, on the other side of the gate. It was a bit of a distance, but it looked like the guy who brought me to the cabin. I couldn't tell for sure. Whoever was in the driver's seat was just sitting there staring at the cabin. After awhile, maybe 30 minutes, I opened the door and waved. A guy got out of the vehicle and it was the same guy who brought me to the cabin. I think his name was something simple and basic like Sam Stone. And Sam had a big bag in his arms."

"A rope, some duct tape, and a blowtorch, no doubt," Bob said semi-serious, but his big grin at the end of the sentence gave away his true intentions.

"As it turned out, he brought me breakfast. Eggs. Bread. Bacon. The works. He then proceeded to make me breakfast."

"Nice guy."

"Shocked the hell out of me." I looked surprised and then complained, "Unfortunately for me, he was an *awful* cook. He used lots of lard and fried the eggs pretty crisp, but I was really hungry and grateful for his kindness."

I continued, "So, we cleaned up and he drove me about half-way up Pikes Peak. He said that the following day was the Race to the Clouds when there was a big all-day race involving cars and motorcycles, and tonight was the only day you can camp on the mountain. So I did. Ends up I partied with a group of new friends and I drank way too much wine. And the effect of the wine was amplified by the high altitude. So, I woke up to a hell of a hangover, and it was freezing cold to boot! I sobered up enough to watch some of the racing and then caught a ride back to Denver and the airport."

"Not a very long adventure."

"I was pretty exhausted. I never really slept the entire time I was there and I knew I hadn't thought the trip out very well. For a while it was exciting being spontaneous, but in retrospect I think I was really lucky that something bad didn't happen to me. I was ill-prepared and naïve. So, I hopped on a flight for home on the Fourth of July. The whole flight home I watched all of these colorful silent explosions below the plane. That was really cool."

"And you were lucky to be alive."

"Lord knows I was pretty clueless back then, and a feather in the wind." I paused for a bit as I think about that earlier adventure. "It was a good learning experience though. I learned to travel light and be prepared. Since then, I always study about where I'm going. Read guidebooks, look at maps."

"Did you do that for this trip?"

"Well, I've done a couple of road trips before, so as long as I have a map, I'm good to go. Candy and I once drove to Yellowstone and the Grand Tetons via Route 90 for a few weeks. Then, a year later, we drove to California taking Route 40." I paused to think a moment, "I think I was on the road that time for 99 days. We took my VW Beetle, a two-man tent, and about $200. We stayed with my sister in Cucamonga for a month and worked to get enough money to continue the trip. Candy worked the register at a Circle K, and I welded heavy-duty metal shelves. Tough work. Really hot and there was lots of grease and grime. Then, it was back on the road. We'd camp a few days and then stay at a hotel for a hot shower and good night's sleep. That summer, we hit most of the big National Parks: the Grand Canyon, Sequoia, King's Canyon, and our final stop, Yosemite. Our goal was Crater Lake in Oregon, but we were running out of money and I needed to get home to go to school. So, we high-tailed it home."

During my storytelling, I didn't include that Candy and I had stopped many times along the way, enjoying the sights and really experiencing the locations. I had hoped this excursion would have been similar, more experiential and less gung-ho travel, however my travel companion was eager to get home.

"Well, I guess it's good to know I'm with such an experienced Road Warrior behind the wheel."

"With quirky bathroom habits," I smiled.

Bob laughed, "We all gotta shit. Some of us are a little more anal retentive than others."

"I guess that's one way to put it," I had to laugh at myself. It was hard to believe I had wanted to push him off a cliff a day earlier. Apparently, my venting had relieved the tension between us, as we both seemed more relaxed today. As Friedrich Nietzsche said, "What doesn't kill you makes you stronger." From my perspective, our traumatic argument the day before seemed to have made our friendship more resilient, our bond more durable.

We had been making good time that morning, as we were already well into Arizona, driving along a short 30-mile stretch on Route 15 between the Utah and Nevada borders. By my calculations, we would easily make Las Vegas for lunch.

Chapter 20

Letting Go

Shortly after crossing the Nevada border, we spied a sign indicating that Las Vegas was only 80 miles away, so we planned to stop there for lunch around 1 p.m. It was my shift behind the wheel and I was still quite exhilarated by my earlier encounter with nature while hiking at Zion National Park. We were listening to a Classic Rock station, which meant we heard our share of music from the '60s and '70s; this was entirely tolerable depending on the song selection. So far, we had been lucky and heard a lot of Beatles, Stones, Zeppelin and Doors.

I began to realize that our road trip would soon be coming to a close. In fact, it was more than feasible that we could reach our final destination, Palm Springs, by early evening. I think that Bob could sense the end of the trip was at hand as well. Maybe that's why we both seemed to make more of an effort to get along so we could thoroughly enjoy the last leg of the journey.

For the first time all week, I felt more relaxed and focused about my concerns at hand. For me, one of the key goals of the trip was to spend time assessing where I was in my life as I entered my forties, and determine my next steps concerning my romantic relationships and my current career choice.

Within the brief period we had been on the road, I felt I had made fairly good progress within this process. I was making an honest assessment of my concerns, then asking Bob for his perspective as a trusted friend and confidant, and finally spending some to reflect and process the information as we traveled down the road. Progress had been made, yet I still had a few things to work out.

"Y'know I really stress out about what I plan to do with my life," I began sharing with Bob. I turned down the radio so it was barely audible in the background.

"No!" He feigned surprise with a broad gesture of placing his hands on his cheeks, thus emphasizing his response. I had to laugh. I deserved that. When was I *not* stressing over something?

"No kidding, right?"

"Hey Mr. Tension, you and 'stress' are synonymous in my mind."

"Well anyway," I continued. "My point is that I have always worried about the Big Questions in life and I have always labored over them. Why am I here? What's my destiny? What should I be doing with my life? I stressed over what to study in college, what career to choose. I'd constantly obsess over these questions, journal about them, talk to friends about them, on and on and on. Well, anyway, to make a long story short."

"Too late, Mr. T," Bob said with a snicker.

"You're right," I said. I had been taking the scenic route to get to my destination. "I know, get to the point, Nejman. Well, it just occurred to me: What if I'm here just to *have fun*?"

I got more enthusiastic as I continued to make my point, "What if I'm here simply to experience all that life has to offer? To enjoy nature and culture and just travel. Have new experiences. In short, to live a life worth living."

Before I continued, I took a deep breath and let it out slowly. "No worries about what I need to accomplish within a career, no lofty goals." All of a sudden, I felt really wonderful, like I had this big weight drop off my shoulders. I smiled and a Zen-like calmness came to my voice. "I need to stop over-thinking everything. Reduce stress. Stop sweating over all the small stuff."

"Live in the moment."

"Right! No worries about tomorrow or regrets about yesterday. Just enjoy what is now." I began to get pumped up again and it was hard to contain my growing enthusiasm, "Hell, there are times that I do more in a week than most people do in a month. Go to events, concerts, films, museums, all kinds of cultural activities; sometimes several things in one day. I'm always in motion. I'll sleep when I die!"

"Sounds like an ideal way to avoid commitments," Bob said to me with stunning clarity. He was right. If I was always in motion, I wouldn't have time to reflect on where I am and what I want for the future.

What had felt right for me, suddenly felt wrong.

A bit bewildered as I thought about it, I muttered, "True."

If I was going to change and become a better person, a better partner, I'd also need to feel comfortable with committing to someone and seeing a future with her.

I also needed to take my professional life more seriously, to become more committed to my career and more mindful of the choices was making, or not making.

I started processing my thoughts out loud, using Bob as a sounding board again.

"But, it's like the interview question where your potential employer asks, where do you see yourself in five years," I began. "I always hated that question. I didn't want to know what was in-store for me in five years. I want to see what life offers up and go with the flow."

I continued, practically arguing with myself, "There's no point in making plans anyway. No matter how much you think you want to be a writer, or whatever, it doesn't matter because so much of the decision is out of your hands. You may have just written a great book, but if you're not in the right place at the right time, it'll never see the light of day."

I sensed Bob was hearing, *Blah, blah, blah.*

"Hey, if you're happy living in the moment, then that's what you should be doing," he said. I think he was simply placating me, praying for silence.

I paused for a bit and looked down the road. I couldn't tell if he was sincere or challenging me to think this *live in the moment* philosophy through and perhaps, make a change. Maybe it was time to set a five-year goal and work toward something I wanted instead of simply reacting to what life provided me. As I contemplated his comment further, I took a sip from my bottle of water.

"I am pretty happy for the most part. But, I have always thought about writing for a living. It just keeps resurfacing in my fantasies."

"Maybe it's time to consider some new dreams," Bob said. "What was important to you as a young man isn't necessarily important to you now at 40."

"Good point. I had stumbled into my job at Harper, yet it seems like a really good fit for me. Maybe it was all meant to be. I surely wouldn't have stayed there for 15 years if there wasn't something I really liked about it."

"Like a regular paycheck and benefits, for instance?" Bob said, teasing my safe, fiscally conservative side.

"And lots of time off to travel!" I quickly offered up. "Like I said before, time off is important to me."

I began to count on the fingers on my right hand with a quick review, "Fridays off in the summer. Ten-day holiday break in the winter. Freedom to travel during the off-season. I get to work with wonderful people who I truly enjoy being with, many of whom are like family to me. And best of all, I get to meet amazing celebs from the entertainment field. How many people do you know whose job is to take Jay Leno to dinner before he performs? Or have a beer with Dr. Benjamin Spock and watch the World Series after a lecture?" In earlier years, I had experienced both contacts.

I heard myself and it seemed to me as if I was working awfully hard to justify my current situation.

"Fair enough," Bob said. "Your current job certainly has its benefits."

It did, I thought to myself. It was certainly a better-than-average job. I wasn't doing something mundane or tedious, like developing advertising slogans for toilet paper, or selling life insurance. Those were jobs that were — in my mind — nothing more than that: Jobs. They were unfulfilling distractions on your way to retirement. Ways to pay the bills, and nothing more.

I thought for a moment and shared, "As long as I'm not *average*, though." I said the word "average" with great disdain, as if it were an incurable disease. "Not me. I want more out of life. You know what I mean?"

"Hey, look who you're talking to," Bob said with a smile. "My greatest fear in life is to be boring. It ain't going to happen!"

I nodded in agreement.

"Maybe I need to look at writing as a hobby for now," I said. "Work on writing projects as they materialize, and if and when the opportunity presents itself, I can transition into something more significant later."

Bob looked at me, smiled, and nodded in agreement.

Decisions made and career choice settled for now! I checked it off my mental checklist and pursued the final, and most important, personal crisis to address while on this trip.

"I guess the only problem I still really need to deal with is my love life; it's quite a mess. As my buddy Michael Kardas said, I need to sit in my shit for a while and sort this all out."

Bob looked impressed. "Good advice."

Kardas, a tall, athletic, talented freelance photographer, was part of a Party Posse we began in the 1980s, and one of my closest friends. Like Bob, he was colorful, creative, and completely unfiltered with his always-accurate, yet blunt, advice. It was funny how I seemed to befriend people with similar personalities, but then again I guess that's what a best friend does, tells you what you need to hear because they love you enough to care.

"Yep. I was ready to leap into another relationship shortly after Jennifer and I split, and Kardas brought up a good point: After so many women, maybe it's not them, it's me."

"Good observation. What do you think?"

"I think he's right. I've made some poor choices. Stayed in relationships I shouldn't have, simply because I was afraid to be alone."

Bob nodded in agreement, "Being alone is scary."

Before I continued, I took a deep breath. I was about to share out loud, what I had only thought about on my hike. "I also realize that I need to make a change in myself; to become a better person and a better partner. And, ultimately, I need to be okay with taking a risk and making a commitment to someone."

"Making a commitment, now *that's* scary," Bob said with a chuckle, realizing that this was my romantic Achilles heel and the source of my greatest anxiety.

"Well, it's not going to be easy for me; all of these changes. But, I know its something I need to do."

"Seems like you're really working things out for yourself," he said. "Maybe you should take some time to think about what you need to change about yourself and what you want in a partner."

He paused, thought for a moment, and then continued, "And most importantly, you need to let go of the past before you can move forward with your life. Hell, if you keep looking in the rear view mirror, you can't drive forward."

Although his point was spot on and relevant, the way he tied it to my current situation of driving somehow seemed cheesy to me, like a lame Hallmark card designed to encourage someone.

"And, what a relevant metaphor," I teased him.

Bob responded with a smug nod. His point was well made and almost poetic.

He was right. I needed to truly let go of Jennifer and move on.

As I thought about this, after a few moments a state of calm gradually came over me. This all made sense. I looked out my open window and bathed my face in the bright, warm sunlight. The wind blew back my hair and I felt a sense of relief. The road ahead was free and clear, no construction or traffic jams in sight. Life was good. All was well.

This feeling of contentment and tranquility felt familiar, but it had been a long time since I had experienced it, perhaps decades. This sensation reminded me of my youth, a time of discovery and new experiences. I thought of one time in particular, a day that my memory recalled with such vivid detail, that I almost felt as if I were there again. I began to smile and let out a chuckle.

"What's so funny?" Bob asked.

"I was just thinking about a time when I was young. I was maybe thirteen or fourteen. My buddy and I had scored a cheap bottle of wine from a convenience store near my house. We convinced some woman — she was pretty young, barely legal — to buy us a bottle and in return we would give her an extra five bucks. She did and we snuck the bottle in a brown paper bag to a field next to a nearby public pool. It was early summer, warm and sunny. We laid back on some freshly cut grass and took turns chugging the wine. I think it was MD 20/20. Mogen David, what we called Mad Dog."

"The good stuff," Bob said facetiously. I smiled.

"We drank it fast and we caught quite a buzz," I continued. "There was loud music playing at the pool; something off of Deep Purple's *Machine Head*. 'Highway Star' or maybe 'Space Truckin',' and it played above the screams of the kids splashing around. My buddy and I were so young and into the moment. No baggage. No regrets. No expectations. No real plans for the future. Our slates were clean and the whole of our lives ahead of us. We were just enjoying the moment, enjoying the day. And, I can vividly remember how fucking great that felt.

Laying on the grass, pleasantly buzzed and laughing at the sun."

Nodding, I smiled and looked out the window, and then repeated softly to myself, "Just laughing at the sun."

I took a deep breath and soaked in the moment, recapturing that feeling of freedom and letting go.

After a moment I continued, "Hell, we were *excited* about what was coming next in our lives. Not anxious, not afraid. There were no complications, no worries, and lots of time."

"Of course! When you're young, you got nothing to lose," Bob said, his voice very calm and soothing. "As you get older, taking risks gets harder to do. Mistakes eat up precious time. And time starts to fly by!"

Looking out the window at the passing scenery, Bob thought for a moment and then he turned back to me. "It's like this exhibit I saw in the Museum of Science and Industry years ago. There's this big metal funnel-like object and you take a ball bearing and roll it along the outer ring. As it approaches the hole in the center, it picks up speed and goes faster and faster and faster. Then, suddenly, it disappears into the hole. It's gone."

"Like life," I said soberly.

"Like life," he agreed.

We both sat imagining that visual, lost in our thoughts, and sharing a rare relaxed moment together. Since my threat to toss him off the cliff, Bob had experienced a perceptible metamorphosis. He had become more amicable, easygoing, and understanding of my needs. We were actually having a nice conversation, free from analysis, anxiousness and expletives; a reflective moment shared between two friends.

"Enough of all this introspective shit! I'm hungry, let's fucking eat!" Bob suddenly declared with a broad smile and a zealous gleam in his eye.

Or, maybe not! Like a traffic light blinking yellow to red, Bob had gone from pleasant to impatient in an instant. *Nothing like traveling with an emotional strobe light*, I thought.

"C'mon, snap out of it," Bob playfully barked at me, sounding eager to rally for the last leg of the trip. "We need to focus on my getting home to Palm Springs. I say we seek out an all-you-can-eat buffet in Vegas and do some serious damage."

I barely had time to nod in agreement when he turned the volume knob on the radio to the right, turning up Paul Revere and the Raiders singing their hit, "Kicks."

Actually, their song "Hungry" would have been more appropriate for the moment and our pursuit of a buffet, but I wasn't about to complain, as it was certainly better than some pathetic Top 40 earworm ditty like Styx's "Come Sail Away" that had been a source of torture earlier in our trip. It's funny how music can help make a moment better, and the soundtrack for our trip was getting better by the minute.

Chapter 21

Vegas and Memories of Les

Our big yellow truck pulled into Las Vegas at 1 p.m. I had been to Vegas before, but at night, when the lights were so bright and colorful that they lured gamblers like mosquitoes to a bug zapper. During the daylight, it didn't seem as impressive.

There were lots of casinos and options for all-you-can-eat buffets, but Bob encouraged me to pull off at one of the newer establishments just off the road, making it an *easy in-easy out* surgical buffet strike for us. We parked our vehicle and walked toward the main entrance that had a big bold banner over the doorway advertising their "24/7 all-you-can-eat-buffet!"

Once inside, we walked through a sea of slot machines, all of which were making a cacophony of electronic sounds, and every so often, we'd hear a jackpot, signaled by the loud metallic clinking of coins emptying into the tray. I'm not a gambler, but it was easy to see how mesmerizing, enticing and addictive this environment could be to a risk-taker with a pocketful of coins.

I was stiff from driving and we were both glassy-eyed from

being on the road for so long. Bob and I both needed nourishment, and I was desperate for a caffeine fix.

Just as one might expect, the casino floor plan was designed so that you had to master a maze of slot machines, before you could reach the island oasis of food.

As promised, Bob picked up the tab for lunch and we eagerly took our clean white plates to the buffet to pile them up with everything from a wide variety of salad *fixin's* to rare roast beef at the carving table.

"The salad bar looks great," Bob said as he eyed the rows upon rows of items to choose from ranging from different types of salad greens, to a significant selection of toppings and vegetables.

"Eating healthy sounds good to me," I said as I grabbed a pair of metal tongs to collect bits of freshly cut and washed red leaf lettuce. "Let's grab a salad and come back with a fresh plate for hot items." I was already neatly organizing my salad in my mind.

"Sounds like a plan," Bob agreed, filling his plate with romaine and green leaf lettuce fragments.

Our competitive nature came out as we both strived to fill our plates as high as possible without anything toppling over. Bob's plate looked the most interesting, as his use of dramatic color contrast the reds of the tomatoes with the greens of his lettuce and asparagus stalks. But I think I had the tallest salad between us, thanks to my carrot stick scaffolding providing a solid foundation.

We grabbed a vacant table amongst a fairly congested lunchtime crowd. Most people were chowing away on grub, while a number of die-hard gamblers started selecting numbers for the Keno cards stacked at each table while nursing their beverages.

"You gamble?" I asked Bob as we delved into our leaning towers of salad.

"The House always wins, so it's not really gambling. I just don't bother," he replied sorting through the salad for just the right forkful of veggies and dressing.

"Me neither. When I come to Vegas, I plan on spending X dollars on entertainment. And to me, losing money isn't very entertaining."

"Have you been here before?"

"Couple of times. I had a buddy who worked at a casino and visiting him took a lot of stamina."

"How so?"

"One time, he picked me up from the airport with a to-go coffee mug filled to the brim with a lethal cocktail, and then we proceeded to stop at every bar between the airport and his condo for refills. After the third or fourth bar, you get pretty sloppy."

I ate a forkful of lettuce, not wanting to fall too far behind Bob's lead.

"Then, we partied at his place and when I was ready to hit the hay, he announced that we had to get moving because he was late for work," I said and then swallowed another forkful of lettuce. I licked my teeth, clearing away stray bits of green, and continued, "So, while he worked at a the blackjack table , I walked around the casino. The last time I visited him, I had been up for 28 hours straight."

"You win anything?"

"I played the slots and parlayed my fifty bucks into about $350 within a couple of hours. Then, I went to roulette wheel and lost it all within minutes, minus ten bucks I saved to buy breakfast. It really sucked! If I bet red, it came up black. If I bet even, the winning number was odd. Easy 50-50 bets and I always lost. So, I ended up hanging out at the restaurant eating steak and eggs and drinking a bottomless cup of coffee until I had to catch my early morning flight."

I wolfed down a few more forkfuls of food. "My friend was such a trip. He was Italian and I think he was somehow connected to the Mob. As we drove from the airport, he looks over at this mountain range and says, 'You'd never guess how many bodies you'd find up there.' "

"Really?"

I nod. "And then, he offered to take care of Candy, if I

wanted, he knew some guy. Candy and I had just gotten divorced, so he figured I was bitter. I thanked him for the offer, but I wasn't about to have Candy offed."

"Does he still work at a casino?"

"I dunno," I said, and then whispered, "I think he went missing years ago. I never heard back from him. I could only guess that he messed up somehow, maybe went into serious debt."

"And now he's up in the mountains?"

"That's my guess."

Looking up from my plate, I spied an Elvis look-alike who resembled The King during his heftier later years. He was probably not a professional Elvis impersonator, although he was sporting a jet-black pompadour hairstyle, flashy sunglasses and mutton-chop sideburns. He even had a bit of a snarl as he reviewed the buffet's ample gastronomical choices.

"Hey, isn't that Les?" I said softly to Bob.

"Who?" Bob's head bolted up as he searched the crowd.

"Wasn't that the name of the surgical hermaphrodite from the Annie Sprinkle show we saw?"

Annie Sprinkle was a porn star-cum-performance artist who identified herself as a Post Porn Modernist back in the fall of 1990, when Bob and I had witnessed one of her events. She had embarked on a self-proclaimed *Anti-Censorship* series of shows designed to challenge community standards. Bob and I had scored front row seats for her *Annie Sprinkle's Sex Education Class* at a venue called Lower Links on Clark Street in Chicago. If there was one thing we shared in common, Bob and I both appreciated erotic, offbeat, bizarre events.

"Oh, yeah," Bob smiled. "Les!"

We both knew the Elvis look-alike wasn't actually Les, but he had triggered memories of that curiously strange evening.

"Remember when Annie came out in that skin tight white nurse's uniform wearing stilettos and a bustier?" I snickered like a horny school boy.

"Her huge titties looked like they were going to burst out of that outfit!" Bob said and then he recalled a few highlights from her lecture and slideshow.

As part of her Sex Education Class lecture, Annie had shared images of a wide variety of graphic sex acts conducted with some of her clients who were burn victims, paraplegics and amputees. Since she was informing us about the wide variety of terms related to sex and sexuality, she then talked about transvestites, cross-dressers, and finally, hermaphrodites. And lo and behold, she said there was as a surgical hermaphrodite in the audience named Les, who she proceeded to bring up to the stage.

Enter Les who looked like a sleepy, heavily-tattooed, beefy Elvis. Les was originally a woman who went through a sex-change operation and decided to keep his female genitalia. A penis was constructed from skin taken from his thighs and buttocks. The penis was a hollow flap of skin that could be made erect by inserting a hard, plastic tube inside it. Testicles were created using saline sacks, which hid his vagina just behind them. We knew all of these intimate details because Les had disrobed and Annie had walked us through these physical modifications while he sat on an examining table.

To me, the experience was more compelling than shocking, although it was quite precarious sitting in the front row only a few feet from the action.

"Les was all tatted up," I recalled. "Didn't he have all of these directions on his bod, like 'twist here' and 'prod' there? Helpful hints for a potential sex partner."

"Yeah, he had a whole lotta ink," Bob said just before stuffing a forkful of lettuce into his mouth. While he chewed, he nodded, recalling more details about that evening.

"The show ended suddenly though, didn't it?" Bob continued. "Annie was going to perform a *Boob Ballet* but management stopped the show."

I swallowed a mouthful of broccoli quickly so I could insert, "The police were supposedly at the door because some guy fainted in the back of the room and paramedics needed to do their thing. It seemed awfully suspicious to me."

"That was bullshit," Bob shook his head and smiled. "I think it was just a convenient way to end the show before things got really weird."

I nodded in agreement and the motion accidently expelled a few pieces of broccoli off my fork and on to the tabletop. Bob took notice that I didn't eat the broccoli from the table, only from my salad plate.

He looked at me incredulously, "Aren't you going to eat that?"

I looked at the stray broccoli with disdain, "What are you nuts? I'm not going to eat that!"

As I stared at the lone green crowns, I could only imagine the germ infestation left behind by the disgusting, damp rags used to wipe down the tables. Certainly there could now be some Super Germ perched on the broccoli just waiting to attack my colon!

"That's perfectly good food," Bob said. "You're really being silly."

With that, he took his fork, speared the broccoli on the table and promptly deposited it in his mouth and chewed it.

I could barely disguise my urge to hurl.

"To each his own, I guess," I managed to say, suppressing my gag reflex. Bob might as well have swallowed a live cockroach.

We had polished off our salads and wanted some hot food.

"So what do we do, leave the dirty plates here and grab clean ones?" I asked, not sure of proper buffet protocol.

Bob nodded and I followed his lead to the carving table. The roast beef looked rare and enticing. A stack of juicy, red meat looked really appealing at that moment. We grabbed a baked potato and a dollop of sour cream each, to fill out our plates. By the time we returned to our table, our dirty plates had magically disappeared.

"Boy, wouldn't it be nice to have someone clean up after you at home like this?" I said, never fond of doing dishes after preparing a big meal. Bob nodded in agreement as he savored his first slice of roast beef.

"Oh man, that's nice!" he said. "I may need to go back for seconds."

I bit into some roast beef and quickly followed it with a forkful of baked potato, smothered in butter and salt. This was easily the best meal we had had on the road.

"Y'know at work I teach these leadership classes for our student leaders each year, and one of my exercises is to ask them to write their own obituary."

"Really?" Bob laughed. "That's weird, isn't it?"

"Sort of, I guess. It helps them to visualize how their lives will be summarized in the end. What do they want to achieve and how do they want to be remembered? What will their legacy be?"

Bob nodded and smiled, "Okay."

"How do you want to be remembered?" I asked him, really curious about his response.

Bob took a minute to finish chewing his food and to give my question some serious thought, "I guess that I want to be remembered for being really good at what I did, that I spent my life to become the best I could, to understand myself and be accountable."

Bob's thoughtful answer surprised and impressed me. I had imagined that he would have wanted to be known as a really influential and admired painter.

"That's really a great answer," I admitted. "I really like it."

"What about you?"

"I want to be known for living a life worth living. For having had a real lust for life. To have traveled the world, enjoying culture and art at every turn. And, to have been a life-long learner," I said, having given this response a lot of thought over the years. As the instructor for these workshops, I had always modeled the behavior I sought from my students and went first with my response when we did this assignment.

As I thought about it, I continued, "Y'know, I've learned a lot from you."

Bob looked pleased and then surprised. "Really?"

"Yeah, by working with you on several of your Bizzarte events, I learned how to creatively market an event; how to give it an angle that attracts press coverage and make great copy. Then, I applied what I learned to events like with the *World's Worst Film Festival Goes to the Beach*, or my *To Die For* photography exhibits. I successfully secured lots of media coverage and it's thanks to your inspiration."

I referred to one of the programs I developed at Harper, the *World's Worst Film Festival*, where we showed a bunch of goofy Frankie Avalon and Annette Funicello beach movies that cost next to nothing to rent and we often packed the house. We also received coverage in all of the Chicago newspapers, while an earlier version of our *World's Worst Film Festival*, featuring celluloid disasters such as *Terror of Tiny Town*, *They Saved Hitler's Brain*, and *Plan 9 From Outer Space*, actually secured national press. In addition, I promoted a series of cemetery photography shows in a variety of venues and packaged them as *To Die For: A Celebration of Cemeteries and the Lighter Side of Death*. The title begged for coverage and plenty of people came to see my pictures of celebrity gravesites from all around the world.

"Well, I'm glad my *shtick* was of some help to you," Bob laughed.

The next thing I said was sincere and heartfelt, yet it came out kind of sappy.

"And, I really appreciate all of your insights and feedback on this trip. You've really been a big help to me. I appreciate the chance to talk out my problems. So, thanks."

I don't think Bob was used to receiving compliments, so he dodged my comment using humor.

"Even when I torture you over your bathroom habits?" he joked.

"Even when you torture me," I said with a smile.

After an awkward pause, he said, "I still can't believe we're such good friends."

"Why's that?"

"I dunno, you're just *so clean*." He said the word "clean" as if it were a vile, incurable disease.

"We all have our crosses to bear," I said with a shrug.

We had both cleaned off our plates. I was washing down my food with a glass of ice water as Bob looked around the room trying to locate something, but I couldn't tell what. I was pleasantly full, but not overwhelmed.

After looking in every direction, Bob located the dessert table, however I was not in the mood. I suggested we maybe stop for coffee and pie in a couple of hours and let this meal digest. He agreed.

"So, you wanna go gamble?"

I halfheartedly responded, "Nah."

"You wanna go see Wayne Newton?"

"Nah."

"Good! Me neither."

"Well what do you wanna do?"

"You have to ask?" Bob then quickly commanded, "Let's hit the road! I wanna get home!"

"Sounds good to me," I stood up out of my chair and tossed him the keys. "Your turn."

We headed back to the parking lot, carefully navigating the labyrinth of noisy, electronic slot machines. We observed a strange mix of retirees, White Trash, and a few businessmen pumping the slots with coins with hopes of hearing the clinking of their metallic winnings. I, for one, was grateful ours was a brief visit. After the dramatic, natural beauty of Zion National Park, this neon-lit, noisy adult playground was very unappealing. For me, authentic always trumped artificial. Besides, it was time to get back to the road and to our Final Destination — not unlike the countless elderly who congregate there – God's Waiting Room: Palm Springs.

Chapter 22

Surviving The Expedition of Death

We returned to the highway and as navigator, I pulled open the road atlas and alternated my attention between the maps for our current state, Nevada, and our upcoming one, California. As I studied the maps, I looked at my watch and then the bright sun well overhead. It was just after 2 p.m. with the hottest part of the day yet to come. Coincidentally, we were heading to California's Mojave Desert, just south of Death Valley National Park, home of THE hottest summer temperatures in the whole United States. Now we were still in the month of May and summer was officially weeks away, but that didn't change the fact that it was almost 90 degrees Fahrenheit outside our truck and we had miles of desert to cross at the worst time of the day. To add to my anxiety levels, I noticed that the truck's gas gauge was hovering just above a quarter tank, my plastic bottle of water was nearly empty, and there were no services in sight; none, nada! Apparently, Bob and I were in such a hurry to exit Las Vegas, that we had broken our tradition of gassing up at every pit stop we made to eat or sleep.

As we drove further and further away from the air-conditioned comfort of the Las Vegas strip — a stretch of land with loads of fountains, swimming pools, and refreshing, cold cocktails — the more I felt a pang of despair and doom in the middle of my gut. I could imagine Bob and myself lying on the ground on the side of the road, next to our broken down truck, with a kettle of vultures circling above us, as they patiently waited for our flesh to bake to a golden brown by the hot midday sun.

I turned to Bob, "You didn't happen to bring any suntan lotion with you by any chance?"

"No, why?"

"The sun feels hot and we're approaching the desert," I said matter-of-factly.

"I can put on the air-conditioner, if you want."

"No, no that's okay," I said, concerned about the potential for a breakdown caused by over-heating. "Just to be safe, maybe we shouldn't put too much strain on the engine or waste fuel by using the air."

"Okay," Bob said nonchalantly, unaware of the potential doom that awaited us just a few more miles down the black asphalt, which I determined was just a few degrees cooler than molten lava.

There was a strange absence of road kill on this stretch of road. I could only imagine that a stray Gila monster could burst into flames as soon as its black, clawed foot touched the asphalt!

I quickly calculated our estimated arrival time at the next nearest town, the appropriately named Baker, was a little more than an hour away. *Surely we could make that destination safely,* I thought to myself, trying to sound convincing to my already freaked out conscious.

The sky was fairly clear with hardly a wisp of a cloud to offer even the faintest protection from the intense solar rays beating down upon our vehicle. I offered a silent prayer, hoping the mechanics that prepped this truck were particularly attentive to its cooling system and had used an ultra-premium radiator coolant, a special formula that not only sealed leaks as they occurred but scoffed at extreme temperatures.

As we continued down the road, the wind was beginning to heat up, like a hairdryer on its highest setting. I could feel the moisture on my skin slowly evaporate and I became hyper aware of how little saliva remained in my mouth. All I could see around us was barren land with only a sprinkling of dry brownish-green brush, and absolutely no signs of life. *What the hell do we think we're doing,* I thought to myself, not in a calm voice, but one with building panic. *Why didn't we leave earlier in the day or plan to travel through the desert at night? Why did I ever let Bob talk me into this Expedition of Death?*

Bob looked at me with concern, "You okay? You look kind of stressed."

I tried to muster enough saliva to speak, but my voice sounded dusty, "Just hot, I guess."

I had been saving the last few drops of my warm bottled water for the heart of the desert, but I needed something to quench my thirst, even if for only a few moments.

Bob noticed my empty bottle. "You thirsty?"

He dug into a small knapsack he kept between us and pulled out a fresh bottle of water.

"I have a couple of bottles of water left. I haven't been very thirsty. Take it!"

I couldn't believe how much I desired this transparent, odorless, tasteless liquid! I opened the bottle and took a long swig. Instantly, I felt refreshed and relieved. My confidence grew. *Damn the oven-like heat! Baker it is! We can make it to this oasis,* I thought. *Once there, we can replenish the petrol, allow the engine to rest, and find liquid refreshment. Then, on to Barstow and beyond!*

Even though I felt some relief, my anxiety still taunted me to keep an eye on my wristwatch as well as on the mileage signs to Baker. Minute by minute, mile by mile, I counted down the upcoming hour and approximately 60 miles to our destination. In my mind, I marked the halfway point and waited patiently for us to get there. We had some time to kill and the radio offered no palatable distraction. *So conversation it is,* I thought.

I perused the topics list in my mind and tried to find something interesting to discuss, yet emotionally neutral. Drama reduction was definitely an important consideration now that we were getting along so well.

"So Bob, are you working on anything interesting these days? Painting, that is."

Bob was deep in thought and it looked like my question startled him a bit. He took a deep breath, allowing himself a moment to think, "Nothing at the moment. I planned on taking a break to go on this road trip."

Bob shifted his weight in his seat and sat up straight, the physical strain of sitting still for so many miles over the past four days was taking its toll.

He continued his thought, "You know, Edward is very supportive of my art. It's really freeing to be able to pursue my painting without having to whore myself out to sell it. I want to continue to paint, but I'm thinking I might pursue photography more. It's appealing to capture an image and tell a story quickly, not having to spend days creating it."

"Photography? That's cool."

Bob had experimented with using acrylic paint on some black and white photographs to creatively add color and modify the subject matter. Either I had taken the photographs he used, or a mutual friend of ours – Jami Craig, so it only made sense that he could easily provide the original photos himself.

Staring at the road and feeling the heat made me daydream a bit. I was thinking about Bob, his paintings, and his Chicago apartment/studio next to the elevated train tracks and a platform, where he had claimed to watch clandestine sex between lovers as they waited for the next train. He had a loft-like place where he created his art and held some amazing parties. One of which was for me; a going away party in 1987, just before I left for London for a four month travel abroad program that was work-related. My role was to coordinate cultural programs for a group of 25 students from all over Illinois. It was an amazing opportunity. Bob was kind enough to host a party for me where about 100 of my closest friends, family members and work colleagues came together to wish me well on my upcoming adventure.

"Hey, you know what I was just thinking about?"

Bob looked at me a bit startled, "What?"

"I was just thinking about that wonderful going away party you threw for me before I left for London."

"Oh yeah," he smiled. "That was a lot of fun. Great group of people."

"You bet, practically everyone I knew was there."

In my mind's eye, I could see the group: elbow to elbow people; my closest friends; my mom and dad; colleagues from work, who were practically like family to me; and even, my ex-wife Candy, which was quite the surprise.

I continued, "A truly great mix of people coming together to wish me well." I thought about it for a minute, "It was kind of like a funeral, but I was still alive to enjoy it!"

Bob laughed.

"It was really great of you to host that party," I said to him with the utmost sincerity. "Thank you. It meant a lot to me."

He smiled, "Hey, anything for my Polish pal."

"Not to get all sentimental or anything, but I really miss having you around," I admitted. "Now that you live in California, we don't have any time just to hang out. I used to love having spontaneous days with you walking around your neighborhood, or hitting a nightclub or two." A group of us would hit the nightclub scene some nights, going to hot spots such as Limelight, Medusa's, Berlin, Neo, Smart Bar, and Crowbar. We never waited in any lines and were always treated like celebrities thanks to Bob's eccentric style and get-out-of-my-way attitude. We often hung out in the VIP section of most clubs, along with all of the movers'n'shakers of Chicago. Being part of Bob's posse, always made me feel special, like one of Andy Warhol's Superstars.

"Well I guess you'll just have to come out and visit me more."

"Of course," I said, although I knew it would never be the same. We had been part of a vibrant Chicago crew that had slowly started to disperse as we all grew older and began to settle down. Some of us started families, others simply grew tired of dancing until the wee hours of the night and having to go to work early the next day.

Times change, people change, and that's the way of the world. Change had never come easy for me, but after much reflection during this road trip, I knew it was time for me to change gears and settle down.

Close to Baker, we saw a sign by the road advertising: Breakfast cooked by The Mad Greek, personally, just ahead.

"I'm not sure why anyone would want his food cooked by someone who's either crazy or angry, but it's a possible place to stop," I said. "What do you think? You wanna visit the Mad Greek?"

"It's a *must!*" Bob smiled, mimicking my enthusiasm for highly desirable touristy destinations. Within just a few miles, we would be safely at an oasis that offered the necessities for completing our trip: gas, food and refreshments. It would be our final stop before driving the last three hours to Barstow and beyond!

Our finish line was almost within view and I looked forward to staying in a place that didn't have paper slip on the toilet seat declaring, "Sanitized for your protection."

Chapter 23

The Mad Greek Diner

There was more than a simple sigh of relief from me as we approached Baker, California, the Gateway to Death Valley and the Home of the Largest Thermometer in the U.S. It had felt as if we had survived a perilous journey to hell and back as we entered California on Route 15, and past Funeral Peak, the Devil's Golf Course, and Funeral Mountain. In my mind, we had cheated Death, and now we were about to celebrate our accomplishment over a feast of coffee and pie.

As we pulled off the road, we couldn't miss the restaurant's blue and white striped awning and bold signs, emulating the colors of the Greek flags displayed prominently around the building. There it was, The Mad Greek Diner, advertising espressos, cappuccinos, fresh strawberry shakes, gyros, burgers, and of course, the breakfast special that was only $2.49!

Even though it was toasty outside, I still desired a hot cup of coffee with my piece of pie. It was part of the ritual and the air-conditioning in the restaurant made the experience more than tolerable. We had passed a spinning rack of pies within a refrigerated case as we walked into the dining area. At a glance, I could identify cherry, apple, lemon meringue, chocolate silk, and some kind of cheesecake. In my mind, the decision was already made: Cherry. Only blueberry pie would be finer, but it wasn't on the menu.

Our waitress looked like *a lifer*, someone who had waited tables since her teenage years and never bothered to venture off into any other line of work. Hell, for all I knew, being a waitress in Baker was as good as it got for a townie. Betsy took our order, calling me "honey," and pouring our coffee as quickly as we ordered it. She was a magician when it came to service, without the constant bother of asking us if we needed anything else. A fine tip was in her future.

I chose to have my pie warm, but no ice cream. Bob had apple pie a la mode.

I took a heaping forkful of the pie into my mouth and washed it down with the coffee.

"My, oh my," I said with great delight. I drew an imaginary horizontal line in the air just in front of me. "If this is heaven," I declared. Then, I pointed to a spot about two inches above the line. "Then, this is this pie!" I moaned as if I had just received the best oral sex in history. It wasn't as noisy and over-the-top as Meg Ryan in *When Harry Met Sally*, but the message was clear.

Bob could barely contain a laugh. "You so need to get laid," he joked as he directed a forkful of apple pie and vanilla ice cream into his mouth.

"Now, be careful not to spill any on the table," Bob said in a motherly tone. "I'm not afraid to eat your sloppy seconds."

His comment was met with my tight-lipped glare. "Trust me, there will be no spoils," I deadpanned through clenched teeth.

As we gorged ourselves on pie, I could hardly fathom where we could find room in our stomachs after the buffet lunch in Las Vegas, but there it was and we were barely speaking between bites.

"Refill?" Betsy appeared just as our cups were in need of

replenishing. She filled them and asked if there would be anything else. We simply asked for the check and enjoyed the refreshing, yet not too cold, air-conditioning. A bathroom break was in order as a restaurant's facilities would certainly be preferential to those of a gas station, which was our next scheduled stop.

As we stepped out of the Mad Greek Diner, the heat of the day hit us as if we were opening the door of an oven.

"There's a Texaco next door," Bob noticed. "Should be our last stop for gas before Palm Springs."

We drove all of a matter of a few yards to the gas station next door. While Bob pumped gas, I went inside the mini-mart to score a bottle or two of water for the road. Little did I know what treasure was in store for me.

Chapter 24

In Pursuit of the Holy Grail of

Guilty Pleasures & Heavenly Delights

Just as Ho Hos are my joyful Guilty Pleasure of snack treats, only one fast-food dessert item surpasses them as the Holy Grail of blissful, sugary, heavenly delights. And of all the convenience stores in all of the world, it was this simple Texaco gas station mini-market, next to the Mad Greek Diner, that featured a rare find that one only dreams of in most states.

The Object of My Desire was a two-part proposition. First, I saw the Coke Slurpee machine behind the counter, spinning the syrupy sweet, frozen delight like a dryer whirling wet clothes. Then, next to it, a vanilla soft-serve machine! Combine the two and you have an icy, creamy Coke Float; Nirvana in a 16-ounce cup!

I walked up to the counter and asked the young cashier for a large Coke Float, please.

He looked at me dumbfounded, as if I had asked him to translate *Crime and Punishment* into Mandarin.

"I'm not sure what that is, sir," he replied after a moment. I noticed his nametag and went for a personal appeal.

"Well, Tom, it's no problem," I said smiling, as if we had been friends for many years." I can walk you through it. First, you take some Coke Slurpee and pour it in a cup, maybe a third or so. Then, pour some soft serve vanilla ice cream in, followed by some Coke Slurpee to top it off. It's really easy."

"I'm sorry sir, but I can't really do that. You see we have a charge for the Coke Slurpee and a charge for the vanilla ice cream, but I don't have any idea what to charge for mixing the two."

The brisk wind behind my sails had suddenly disappeared. I was stunned by his denial, but I tried to remain optimistic. If the Allies could win the war against Germany, surely, there was a way for me to negotiate a treaty to combine Coke Slurpee with vanilla soft-serve ice cream in this little emporium in the desert.

"I am more than happy to pay for a large Coke Slurpee AND a large vanilla soft-serve, if you do as I say," I said with a big toothy smile, like a salesman ready to close a deal on a fully-loaded Lamborghini.

"But how would I ring that up?" Tom asked, and all I could think of is how he really needed to be removed from the gene pool.

"Well, if I was on *that* side of the counter, I would ring up a large Slurpee and then, add a large vanilla soft-serve ice cream," I said, my eyes practically pleading for him to comply.

Tom thought for a moment. And then, his eyes showed the dimmest of glimmers as it looked as if he understood the task at hand and my recommendation for the resolution of payment.

"I guess I could do that, sir, although it's not fair to you. You'll be paying far more than it'll be worth."

"That's more than okay with me, Tom. In fact, it will be my pleasure."

He stepped over and grabbed a cup, placing it under the Slurpee machine nozzle and pouring in some frozen Coke.

"That's good, Tom. Now the vanilla ice cream," I said a little jittery. I could almost taste the icy crystals of delight mixing with the creamy vanilla soft serve. I felt like Peter Lorre and Sydney Greenstreet waiting to touch what they believed to be the Maltese Falcon.

Tom completed the task as if he had been an old pro at mixing Coke Floats, or Black Cows, as they were known back home in Chicago.

"With tax, that'll be $2.26, please."

I pulled out my wallet and slapped down a five-dollar bill. Tom gave me my change, but it didn't matter to me. I would have gladly paid twice that for this treat.

I grabbed the cup and placed a straw into the icy concoction. Then, ever so slowly, I brought the straw to my lips. I now knew the satisfaction Indiana Jones must have felt as he placed his hand on a long sought-after antiquity.

I took a long sip as the icy Coke crystals and the vanilla ice cream mixed in my mouth, providing me with liquid refreshment that could only be described as "The Drink of the Gods." As I swallowed the heavenly contents of my mouth, I felt a rush of searing pain strike my brain like a hot poker. *Brain freeze!*

I waited patiently for the pain to subside, and then, like a young boy who hadn't learned his lesson, I repeated the experience again, with the same results. There was a bizarre pleasure-pain connection, yet it was very satisfying and rewarding. After the third attempt, I allowed the frozen heavenly drink to melt more in my mouth before swallowing. This led to a more fulfilling experience for me.

Walking out to the truck, Bob could see I was still in a state of ecstasy.

"Did you get lucky?"

"You have no idea," I said lifting the cup to show him. I then made an imaginary horizontal line in front of me. "If this is heaven," I said and then placed the Slurpee cup a foot above that line. The image was clear. Coke Slurpee Floats were rated in the *Beyond Heaven* range of delights for me. "You like Coke Floats?"

"Nah, I've had enough sugar for now," Bob said without a hint of curiosity to try at least a sip of mine.

Non-believer! Philistine! More for me, I thought. There was no doubt in my mind that I could easily become a Coke Slurpee Float addict should a supply be secured! Lucky for me, and my teeth, this sugary treat was as rare as witty, pithy dialogue in an Adam Sandler movie.

"Hey, I think we're out of water, though," Bob pointed out as I neared the truck. "Could you get a couple of bottles for the road?"

"Sure," I turned around and jogged back to the store. Water may have been a basic need, but this Coke Slurpee Float was the liquid luxury of divine pleasure.

With our bottled water, full tank of gas, and my supreme sugary buzz, Bob got behind the wheel. We pulled away from Baker and headed toward Barstow and beyond. Driving down the road, I noticed that the liquid of my Holy Grail was dissipating and thoughts of a quick return to Baker haunted my mind. I thought to myself, *it's only 20 minutes back, I could go get another Coke Slurpee Float and we could still be in Palm Springs before dark.*

Chapter 25

Siskel and Ebert on Wheels

Even with the governor on the carburetor, it somehow felt like we were flying down the road as we breezed by Barstow and found ourselves within an hour of San Bernardino. Our magical mystery tour was approaching its end, and intimate time together was limited. Soon, I'd be the third wheel as Bob reunited with his Edward.

In some ways, I felt talked out, and in others, I felt like we had barely scratched the surface with certain topics that we normally discussed incessantly; films, for example. Bob and I were both cinema enthusiasts, each of us seeing one hundred or more films a year and always comparing notes, as if we were Siskel and Ebert-wannabes.

"So, last month I saw a few new films," I began the discussion. "Let's see, first Kevin Smith's *Chasing Amy*, which I liked a lot. A kind of Boy meets Girl, Boy falls in love with Girl, Girl turns out to be a lesbian."

"Oh? A documentary about your love life," Bob teased.

"I certainly could relate to it," I forced a smile.

"Didn't see it."

"Okay, well, I also saw *Inventing the Abbotts* with this really great cast," I thought hard for a moment to dredge up all the names. "Hmm, Liv Tyler, Jennifer Connelly, Billy Crudup, and River Phoenix's brother, what's his name?"

"Joaquin."

"Right! Joaquin."

Bob responded once again with, "Didn't see it."

"Okay, well there was one more and I really, really liked it," I said as I tried to recall the name. It was an odd name for a movie, not very obvious. Then, it hit me, "*Grosse Point Blank!*"

"Now, that film I saw," Bob smiled.

"So, what did you think?"

"It was okay," Bob said without a hint of enthusiasm.

"Just okay," I said incredulously. "I loved it! I thought it was really funny. Especially John Cusack's scenes with Dan Aykroyd."

Cusack portrayed Martin Blank, a professional assassin, who has an assignment in a small Detroit suburb, Grosse Pointe, and by coincidence, his ten-year high school reunion is taking place the same weekend. Aykroyd played a competing assassin and Alan Arkin played Martin's therapist. The climax is hysterical as Blank juggles his job, old friends, his therapist, and an old flame portrayed by Minnie Driver.

"Yeah, it was funny, but it didn't really do anything for me," Bob admitted quite blandly.

"Didn't you love the soundtrack?" I began to gush as I rattled off the bands featured, "The Clash, Violent Femmes, The Jam, The Specials, Pixies, The Cure and this great song called 'Go,' but I don't recall the name of the band."

"Yep, the music was definitely fun," Bob nodded.

"I bet Cusack selected the tracks. I think I read somewhere that he used to go to Wax Trax all the time back in the 80s. We probably crossed paths several times and didn't even know it," I said. As a vinyl junkie, it was my weekly ritual to go to the hottest record store in Chicago, Wax Trax on Lincoln Avenue. With each visit, I'd buy at least half-dozen new records, take them home to tape them, and then sell them back for store credit and then, buy more records. It was a vicious cycle, but one I continued to abuse for many, many years.

"Y'know, I haven't seen too many new movies lately," Bob said. "Ed and I watched *Jurassic Park* again a couple of weeks ago. I really love that movie! There's this great quote that Jeff Goldblum's character, Dr. Ian Malcolm, says."

Bob hesitated to reveal the line, just enough to ensure I was listening intently.

"And...." I said, attempting to prod him along.

"Life," he began and then paused for effect. "Finds a way."

Bob smiled with great satisfaction. He obviously loved that quote.

"That line always shakes me up," Bob continued. "It's made a real impact on me because it's so true!"

"Isn't it funny, the lessons we learn in the dark," I said.

Bob looked quizzically at me.

I clarified, "The lessons we learn about life and all, through watching films. In the dark."

"Ahhh," Bob nodded, he got my point. "Not only in the dark, but with strangers," he added ominously.

"I have a journal at home that I jot down 'Lessons I Learned in the Dark,' messages from movies that had a real impact on me," I shared and then thought about a few of my favorite examples. "Like, *It's a Wonderful Life* and the importance of being a good friend to others."

"No man is a failure who has friends."

"Exactly! Or, *Groundhog Day* with Bill Murray and the importance of making each day count."

"Carpe diem!"

"Right! Seize the day," I said. Then I quickly added two more movies with this same theme, "In my mind, *Dead Poets Society* and *Harold & Maude* fall in the same category."

I thought a moment about another film I had listed in my journal, "And of course, there's the great tale about the importance of friendship and one of my all-time favorite films, *The Shawshank Redemption*."

"How about *The Godfather*?" Bob said semi-seriously, and then joked. "There are many lessons about how to get things done by making an offer someone cannot refuse."

"And that using a horse's head will get you quicker results!"

"Now for me, I have found *profound* messages from TV shows," Bob said.

"Really?"

"There's a *Bewitched* episode where Samantha wants to take Darrin to Europe, but he won't have it, if she uses witchcraft. And then she says, 'Well, what if I just give you the memories of going to Europe?' "

Bob paused for a moment, and then continued, "That's so profound. When you think of it, all we have in life are memories. Once the moment occurs, it's gone forever. What a brilliant line. It just goes to show you that you can even learn something from TV."

After a moment, he continued, "Except for *I Dream of Jeannie*, I never learned anything from that show."

"I always liked *Green Acres*. I don't think I ever learned anything from the show, but it was Theater of the Absurd at its best. Offbeat characters and a pig with personality. What more could you want?"

"Oh wait," Bob quickly interjected with bubbly enthusiasm. "There was this really great PBS movie years ago with Bill Bixby called *Steam Bath*. That show really had an impact on me. God is played by this Puerto Rican steam bath attendant, and there's a scene where he says to these various men in the steam bath, give him a headache, give him a heart attack, have a bird shit on his head....and on, and on." Bob looked at me for a moment, "It really emphasized the randomness of life. How things just occur without rhyme or reason."

"Cool! What was it called again?"

"*Steam Bath*."

"Thanks," I said and I jotted it down in my journal.

"It was very clever. At the end, the Puerto Rican attendant reveals himself to be God and freaks everyone out. It was a real White Light moment."

"White light?"

"Yeah, some people believe that when you die you see this White Light that reveals all the secrets of life. Answers to the Big Question," Bob said with a smirk.

"What was my purpose in being on earth? That kind of stuff?"

"Exactly!" Bob confirmed.

After a pause, he continued, "You know, there are three questions I want answered when I see the White Light. First, who shot Kennedy?"

I nodded in agreement.

"Next, how to properly load a dishwasher."

That one made me laugh, "A-men! I can never make everything fit properly!"

"And third, how to talk to parents about their problematic kids at the playground?"

Not having had any children, I couldn't really relate to that one, but I assumed it would be challenging. Again, I nodded.

Then, I thought to myself, what would I want to know about? Obviously for me, I would want to know what my ultimate purpose on earth was, or if I even had one. I wondered if my epiphany, that I was here to simply embrace life and culture, to have fun, was accurate.

"For me, I'd like to know if I had achieved my purpose in life."

Bob rolled his eyes.

"*Oy!* Maybe you were destined to be my lackey and you overachieved," he said with a smirk.

Right, I thought. I was taking the question too seriously. *What would I want to know?*

"Actually, I'd love to know who killed Marilyn Monroe. With her connections to the Kennedys, I've always felt her overdose was a lie."

"Agreed," Bob nodded.

"And, I want to know why smoke alarm batteries always die at 2 a.m.?"

That one made Bob laugh.

After a moment, I offered another thought, "I also wonder if the after-life is like Albert Brooks' film *Defending Your Life*, where there's a Judgment City and your life is assessed. Then, it's decided if you move on or not. Maybe get reincarnated or reach a new level of existence."

"Or, do you just fade to black?"

"Yep, that's certainly an option, I guess," I agreed, but I found that thought very depressing. I might not have been very religious in the sense of practicing Catholicism on a regular basis, as in attending mass weekly, but I did pray and feel there is a Supreme Being. There was hope in my heart that all the talk of a heaven was accurate and we all have a place to hang out for eternity after our stint on earth; an after-hours bar where we could reminisce, tell stories, and flirt with Victoria Secret models with angel wings.

"You know, I really hope there's a heaven," I said. "I like the notion of re-connecting with my grandparents and other relatives, having a chance to meet my ancestors. Seeing if I did them proud."

"I think it would be cool to meet famous people from the past, like Picasso, Shakespeare, and Errol Flynn."

"Now there's a dinner party!"

"With my luck, they'd all be in the VIP section and I wouldn't have access," Bob joked. "No Jews allowed."

"You know who'd I like to meet? Salvador Dali, Groucho Marx, and John Lennon. I think the conversation would be mind-boggling."

"I think it would make my brain hurt," Bob cringed.

A sign near the road indicated that San Bernardino was less than ten minutes away, which meant that we were about an hour away from Palm Springs. That thought really gave me an uneasy feeling in my stomach. It meant that I'd be spending more time with Edward, a man I had only met once before at a gallery show, but who had now become my best friend's partner.

Chapter 26

The Paradise Ranch

We continued on Route 15 to the 215 through San Bernardino, and then we hooked up to Route 10 going east to Palm Springs. The interchange of routes 215 and 10 was a stack of three on and off ramps, the quintessential L.A. visual, as Bob explained.

"That's L.A. for you," he quipped. "Stacks upon stacks of freeways. Out here it's all about the car. As they say, nobody walks in L.A."

Bob was right as he referenced the New Wave band Missing Persons who made that observation back in 1982 and it still rang true in 1997. Of course we were more than an hour east of Los Angeles, but it was the general vicinity.

Driving east on Route 10, the traffic started to get more and more congested. It was 5:30 p.m. and we were in the midst of rush hour traffic as Southern Californians returned home from work, and those on the late shifts, were just leaving for their jobs. Back home in Chicago, the evening rush hour usually lasted from 3:30 p.m. to 6:30 p.m., perhaps later in bad weather. In the greater Los Angeles area, rush hour was pretty much continuous, with somewhat lighter traffic occurring between 10 p.m. and 5 a.m.

As the traffic thickened and closed in around us, I began to feel claustrophobic. Bright red brake lights pulsated in front of us as we stopped and started, stopped and started, inching our way down the road. A black Mercedes Benz, with dark tinted windows, cut directly in front of us without signaling, which caused Bob to suddenly slam on the brakes.

"What. The. Fuck!" Bob didn't appreciate the unannounced lane change. It had been a long, hot day and we were both tired and eager to exit the truck's cab for an extended break.

"What a jerk!"

"What a motherfucking asshole," Bob corrected me. He honked the horn and we both gave the driver a middle-finger salute.

"I have a Theory of Annoying Drivers," I said. "Want to hear it?"

Bob nodded.

"The nicer the car, the bigger the asshole driving it. I'm not sure if it's a sense of entitlement or that they are just in their own little world, but drivers of BMWs, Mercedes, and cars like that, never allow you to merge, rarely use their turn signals, and almost always cut you off."

Bob laughed. "I'll have to keep that in mind and see if it's true for me."

Luckily, the congestion didn't last long. It took twenty minutes to drive about two miles as we crawled along. However, once we drove past Redlands, the traffic eased up a great deal, and once again we were on the open road, cruising along at our designated speed of 55 mph.

This was a stretch of road that I was familiar with – having visited Bob in Palm Desert, where he lived for awhile with his wife Paula and their three kids, and to visit my college friend and talented photographer, Marc Glassman, better known as Marco Photo to those close to him. I usually spent time with Marc each time I visited my sister, Mary.

The radio station we were listening to featured alternative rock, so their playlist was heavy with Nirvana, Red Hot Chili Peppers, Pixies, Pearl Jam and Stone Temple Pilots jams.

As the beginning of STP's "Vasoline" sounded, I yelled, "Turn it up!"

I cranked the volume knob to the right, blasting the speakers.

"If it's too loud, you're too old!" I reminded Bob, although he didn't protest the increased volume. The throbbing bass and driving drums were just the propellant we needed to complete our journey. I screamed along with their lead singer, Scott Weiland and then played air guitar mimicking Dean DeLeo's lead guitar riff. Like a middle-aged version of Wayne Campbell and Garth Algar, Bob and I rocked our heads back and forth in a way that would make Mike Myers and Dana Carvey proud.

As "Vasoline" came to a close, Kurt Cobain's opening guitar strains announced the beginning of "Smells Like Teen Spirit," which were soon joined by the sonic assault of Dave Grohl's pounding drums and Krist Novolselic's pulsating bass. We were now bouncing in our seats with the beat and nodding our heads in perfect synch. We were as giddy as teenagers experiencing their first beers.

Bob and I both joined in on the closing chorus, yelling boldly, practically drowning out Kurt.

As the feedback from Kurt's guitar faded out, a commercial for a local taco joint came on and brought our audio high to a screeching halt. It was one of those amateur productions with irritatingly lame dialogue, probably written by the owner and featuring his wife and her best friend discussing their lunchtime needs. I couldn't turn the volume down quickly enough. It was a bummer of a buzz kill, although it didn't matter much since the white noise of radio static soon began to overtake the signal and we would eventually need to seek a new station or turn it off completely. We both agreed on the latter choice. It had been a long day and the lack of noise was extremely appealing.

Besides, I appreciated some quiet time to think about what to say to Edward. He was now my best friend's partner and I wanted to be sure to make a good impression. The fact that Edward was a retired English Lit. professor from Manhattan College, and a published author and poet, certainly made me more than a tad bit nervous and anxious. I had only briefly met him at the David Leonardis Gallery in November, but it only took moments to see that he was very witty and clever. He reminded me of a modern day Oscar Wilde-type of intellectual and I certainly didn't want him to think of me as Bob's boring friend from Chicago.

As we approached Palm Springs, just miles before the California Route 111 exit, rows upon rows of the towering white windmill-like turbines of the San Gorgonio Pass Wind Farm, Southern California's early attempt at a renewable energy source, came into view. This image would have certainly freaked out Don Quixote and sent him running back to La Mancha! I couldn't help but think of all these turbines as big fans cooling off the desert heat and making Palm Springs a more comfortable place to live, an absurd yet fun notion.

"It won't be long now," Bob announced, I could see he was getting excited about being so near home and his Edward. "We'll soon be at my Tara, the Paradise Ranch."

I smiled to myself as he referenced *Gone With the Wind* while declaring the name of his new homestead. It was rare for Bob to romanticize *anything*. In fact, I could only think of one other instance. The gallery that displayed his work back in the 1980s was called the Pavilion for the Arts on Wells Street, just south of North Avenue. Instead of calling it the Pavilion for the Arts, Bob always referred to it as the *Pah-vee-ahn del Ar-tay*, as if it were an iconic Italian institute for the arts. Now, his humble home with Edward became The Paradise Ranch. His rose-colored glasses were endearing.

We pulled on to Route 111 to North Palm Drive, just west of us was the Agua Caliente Indian Reservation and the mountains of the San Jacinto State Park, and we drove south to North Palm Drive, which turned into South Palm Drive.

Bob was practically gleaming by this time. He was only moments from home and I could see his anxiousness at every light we had to stop for, each delay made him take a deep breath. All of a sudden, every second counted and he was eager to reach home. He reminded me of a four-year-old boy waiting to tear into his presents on Christmas morning.

Soon we came to Mesquite Drive and made a left turn; we passed a few houses. Bob pulled the truck into a short driveway and up to an electronic, solid sheet metal gate.

"Home" Bob said. "Michael, welcome to the Paradise Ranch!"

I looked at my watch and it was just about 6:45 p.m. Then, I looked west and determined there was still at least a good hour before sunset.

Bob leapt out of the truck's cab and bounced to the nearby operational keypad. He tapped in a four-digit number and the gate began to roll open, each section of sheet metal slid into the next, until we had a space wide enough for us to pull in. Bob popped back into the cab, slid the truck into gear and slowly allowed the truck to creep forward, stopping just before a garage door. The driveway wasn't very long, but we were able to move the truck into the driveway with several feet to spare behind us, so the gate could close.

"Wait here," Bob instructed me as he again leapt out of the truck and back to the gate's keypad. He pressed a button and the gate closed behind us. He stepped back into the cab.

"Gimme a few minutes," he said with a smile. "I'd like to say 'hi' to Edward before you come in."

"Sure, no problem," I assured him. "I need a few minutes to collect my things and jot down a few notes."

I had barely spit out the last few words when Bob darted for the front door, which he unlocked and entered with the speed and finesse of a cat burglar.

Chapter 27

Reuniting with Edward

The Paradise Ranch was a traditional Spanish Colonial-style structure, with a light beige stucco façade, an adobe-tiled roof and Sienna-colored trim. The building was a rare two-level home amongst a sea of single level ranches throughout the neighborhood. I believe Bob had said something about building regulations having had changed in recent years to limit homes to only one level due to earthquake concerns.

Six towering palm trees were showcased in the beautifully landscaped front yard. Additional tall palm trees were near the garage, and four bordered the west property line.

A six-foot tall dark brown wooden fence on the east side of the house hid the backyard. Between the solid brick four-foot high wall in the front of the yard, the electronic sheet metal gate, and the tall wooden fence, it was obvious that privacy was of the utmost importance to the owners.

The wooden front door was a bold red, framed with white tiles that had green, leafy decorations on each, another Spanish tradition. Next to the door was a flagpole with a four-foot-by-six-foot rainbow flag, boldly indicating to all that the inhabitants of this abode were gay and proud of it.

Our truck was parked in front of a garage, and above it was a deck with a dark brown canopy providing shade. To the west of the garage, was another garage, which I would later find out was part of a guesthouse.

Interestingly enough, the house stood across the street from a large vacant lot the size of a full block, which looked as if it had gone undeveloped for years. This was a mystery to me as this tony neighborhood was prime for additional housing, or perhaps a small mall of boutique stores.

I pulled out my journal to record that the trip had taken a total of four days, and we had travelled a little more than 2,030 miles. I wasn't about to calculate how many hours of armchair therapy I had shared with Bob, but I knew it was significant. I pulled together all of my possessions from the cab, pushed them into my duffel bag and awaited my invitation to join Bob and Edward.

Within moments, Bob appeared in the front door and waved me in. Leaving the truck's cab, I took my time walking to the front door, allowing a few moments to stretch my legs after being confined for several hours. As I reached the door, Bob held it open for me as Edward stepped up to meet me.

"You remember my Polish, heterosexual friend, Michael," Bob said. Edward gave me a big smile and a warm handshake.

"Welcome to *our* home, Michael," Edward greeted me. "If there's anything I can do to make your stay more comfortable, I hope you won't hesitate to ask."

I had forgotten how tall Edward was, so his height surprised me a bit. We shook hands and I couldn't help but admire his impeccable taste in clothing. Even though he was in casual attire – jeans, sandals, and a loose-fitting white-collared shirt — he looked as if he'd just walked off a photo shoot for a Ralph Lauren ad in *Gentlemen's Quarterly* magazine. Looking his role as a retired English Lit professor, his distinguished white hair was long, and slightly unkempt, with a few independent strands resting on his round, thin, wire-rimmed glasses. He combed back the hairs with his hand. Two large dogs had accompanied Edward to welcome me.

"Edward! It's good to see you again!" I stepped into the vestibule, which was considerably cooler than the warmth of the early evening. Sunset was still more than an hour away so the outside temperature remained toasty.

"Stella! Aristotle! Stay!" Edward shouted out and the two dogs followed his orders immediately.

"Let me introduce you," Edward turned to the dogs. "This is Stella," he pointed to a Great Dane. "And this is Aristotle," he said motioning toward a big, black Royal Poodle. Both dogs were regal looking and well behaved, still I must have looked somewhat startled by their massive size and fervor.

"Don't worry, they're as gentle as can be," Edward assured me. "I'm sure you'll all get along just fine."

Edward stood erect and rubbed his palms as if he were warming his hands.

"You two must be hungry. What do you say we see what's in the fridge."

Edward turned towards the kitchen. As he did, the dogs moved toward me, their noses vigorously sniffing my crotch. This was a common activity when dogs met me for the first time, however with the size of these two, I was more than a bit concerned for the safety and well being of my three amigos.

"Thanks," I said uneasily, struggling to step around the dogs to follow Ed and Bob. I placed my right hand over my crotch and shoved away Stella with my thigh. "I could eat."

We walked into a gourmet kitchen that was modern, stylish and fully functional, with an island in the middle boasting a restaurant-grade stove and a nearby ceramic-tiled workstation. Pots, pans, and cooking utensils hung above the stove on a black wrought-iron rack, just behind a hood providing ventilation. Any chef would find it a pleasure to cook in such surroundings. Edward opened the nearby stainless steel refrigerator and took stock of its contents.

"Let's see, had I known you two were going to be home for dinner, I would have bought some steaks, but I'm sure I can whip something up that you'll enjoy," Edward said as he assessed each shelf. "It looks to me like we have the ingredients for a nice Denver omelet. Does that appeal to you?"

"That sounds great," I said. "I could eat breakfast three times a day."

Bob was in agreement, so Edward pulled out the eggs, some ham, and a bell pepper from the fridge. Then, from a wire-mesh hanging basket nearby, he grabbed a yellow onion.

"I'll get dinner going, Bob why don't you give Michael a tour of the place," Edward said as he started to prep for the meal.

Bob noticed that I still had my duffel bag in hand. "You can put that by the back door. You'll be staying in the guesthouse. I think you'll be very comfortable there."

"Cool!" I liked the idea of having a place to myself that would be private and quiet, especially after almost four days of tight, shared quarters.

"Best of all, it has a private master bathroom that's sound-proofed," Bob teased.

As we walked toward the back patio doors, I couldn't help but marvel at their home. The whole place was impeccably decorated with enough artwork to rival a small museum. The living room had a fireplace with well-stocked bookshelves and a stereo playing continuous classical music. The remaining walls were covered with paintings, etchings, and photography. Several of Bob's more vibrant and dramatic paintings were hung in prominent locations, surrounded by an impressive variety of work by well-known artists including sketches by Picasso and Chagall, as well as a few pieces by contemporary *outsider* artists.

"Wow!" I looked around the room, taking it all in. "This is very, very impressive. I can see why you were in a hurry to come home."

The furniture was a combination of designer pieces, a couple of Bob's painted chairs, and two, soft, brown leather reclining lounge chairs, near the fireplace, that looked incredibly inviting.

"There's the dining room," Bob said pointing to a separate room that jutted out toward the backyard, the windows providing a beautiful view of a pool and garden area. The table was already set with colorful dishes, place mats and glassware, along with four high-back cloth chairs, that were all painted by Bob with a variety of colorful imagery. The room looked ready for a *House Beautiful* magazine photo shoot.

"Let's go outside, I think we'll eat on the veranda tonight," Bob said as he opened two French doors to go out on the patio. We stepped out on to the porch, where there was a table already set for dining, along with four chairs.

It appeared that Bob and Edward were certainly meticulous about decorating details, yet the place looked warm and lived in, not sterile and preserved.

Directly in front of the veranda was a swimming pool with nearby lounge chairs and a lemon tree. To the west, was a small pond filled with about a dozen sizeable and brightly colored koi fish, with a nearby three-foot high rock waterfall. The sound of the running water was soothing and could be heard in unison with the classical music that was playing on outdoor speakers.

Next to the pond was the guesthouse, a small beige-stucco ranch with a deep teal wooden porch. Hanging on the blank outside wall space of the house was a large, colorful portrait of Bob – with a pith helmet, full-beard and round, black-rimmed glasses, circa early 1980s when he resembled the director of *The Godfather*, Francis Ford Coppola – in addition, there was a dramatic Warhol-like painting of the actress Frances Farmer, identical to the tattoo on Bob's right arm, his signature image. Planted in front of the porch was Little Bluestem ornamental wild grass, which had a striking red and bluish coloring and fluffy, reddish white seed heads.

I turned to Bob and sighed, "I can see why you call this the Paradise Ranch. It's all so tranquil and beautiful."

"It's like an all-inclusive resort, with special benefits *pour moi*," Bob said, obviously pleased to be home again. "There's always more than a chocolate mint on my pillow each night."

"Dinner's on!" Edward bellowed from the kitchen. "Robert, give me a hand with these plates, please."

Bob returned to the house and I took a seat at the outside table on the veranda. The four chairs had thick cushions, which felt so much more comfortable than the stiff seats of the truck cab. The table already had four placemats and a Lazy Susan in the middle, complete with a silverware caddy, white paper napkins, salt, pepper, and a small container with a collection of pink and yellow packaged artificial sweeteners.

I identified the music playing as the soothing first movement of "Summer" from Vivaldi's *Four Seasons*, well before the unsettling and dramatic strings later in the piece that evoke a thunderstorm. A light, warm breeze caressed the patio area and for the second time this day, I soaked it all in and took a deep breath, and then slowly exhaled. Not unlike my experience at Zion National Park, I was in a relaxed, pleasant state and truly happy to be alive.

Bob soon arrived with a tray of three, tall chilled glasses of orange juice, followed by Edward with a tray of three plated Denver omelets, and another plate of warm croissants. Like a well-trained serving staff, they delivered their goods and then placed the now empty trays on the unused fourth chair.

Taking his seat, Edward lifted his glass of orange juice, "A toast to our guest Michael."

We all clinked our glasses and sipped the beverage. What I had thought was plain orange juice turned out to be a refreshing Mimosa.

"Yum, Mimosas," I said with a smile, barely separating the two words. "How wonderful. Thank you."

"Having us all together is indeed an occasion for celebration," Edward said as he returned his glass to the table. "I didn't make the croissants fresh, but I did a swell job of heating them up."

Everything looked so good. I politely snagged a croissant and placed it on my plate. Then, I dug into the omelet, which was absolutely delectable. I couldn't help but think: Edward is good-looking, intelligent, rich, AND he can cook, too! Bob had indeed scored the Brass Ring.

"The omelet is delicious, Edward. Thanks."

My compliment was sincere; I had hoped he didn't think I was just sucking up.

"I'm glad you like it," Edward said, I could tell he appreciated my comment. "So, how was the trip?"

Bob and I looked at each other, not only trying to guess each other's assessment but also determining who would respond first.

After an awkward pause, I said, "It was a lot of fun" at the same time Bob, said "It was good."

I looked at Bob a little surprised. *Good,* as a description, is as neutral as saying something is "interesting;" both adjectives allow a lot of room for interpretation. Plus, as challenging as some of the trip was, I felt it had certainly solidified our friendship. I felt a little hurt by his flat response. Even though *it was a lot of fun* as a response was not a resounding rave review of our escapades, it was at least positive.

Bob could sense my offense to his comment and spoke up, "What I meant to say was that the trip was good, with a lot of fun moments."

"Exactly," I chimed in. Bob surprised me. He was acting very cordial as his comment was free from his usual acerbic wit and sarcastic barbs. This personality shift seemed surreal. Either Edward was really a positive influence on him, or he was displaying extra-good behavior to further impress his partner. *Had I been with Bob's evil twin these past four days?*

"Iowa and Nebraska still flat?" Edward continued to facilitate the conversation by asking his questions, this one reflecting his dry sense of humor.

"Oh yeah," I confirmed with a heavy nod.

"An endless sea of corn," Bob added.

"So I'm curious, what did you two talk about for four

days?" Edward said, popping his verbal volley into Bob's and my court.

Bob and I looked at each other. *Where does one begin?* I thought. I smiled and joked, "You know, sports, politics, the usual."

Bob laughed and teased back, "That was us, all right. We must have spent hours analyzing the crisis in the Middle East."

"Well, you are both here safe and sound, and for that, I am grateful," Edward said, picking up his glass. "Another toast. This time to having Robert back home, I really missed you!" Edward lifted his glass in Bob's direction. We all clinked glasses, and then Bob warmly kissed Edward and gave him a hug. I looked away momentarily to allow them a bit of privacy. It was an awkward moment for me as I felt like an interloper.

Edward had acknowledged both Bob and me, so I felt a need to speak up.

"And a toast to Edward. I've never seen Bob so happy," I said with my glass held high. Once again, our glasses met and we went on to finish our meals and drink more Mimosas.

After dinner, we played a game of *Scrabble*, while sipping our vodka martinis. My after-dinner drink of choice was usually a Scotch on the rocks, but I had rarely had a martini and it seemed like the sophisticated cocktail to indulge in that evening.

We talked and talked for several hours about everything from movies and art, to books and travel. Our conversation was lively and I thought Edward was fascinating. Like any good professor, he knew how to frame questions so that he engaged the entire group. It was easy to see why Bob loved him and was so eager to return to the Paradise Ranch. As the two of them interacted, I saw a more amiable and relaxed Bob. He was home again. Mission accomplished.

Chapter 28

Bubbles, Lucy-Style

The moon was visible from our table, and the clear dark sky hosted hundreds of sparkling celestial bodies. It must have been around ten o'clock when I determined that I really needed to call it a night. I thanked Edward for a wonderful evening and Bob walked me over to the guesthouse, making sure I could find everything before crawling into bed.

Bob pulled out a key from under the doormat and unlocked the door, then quickly flipped on a light and the overhead ceiling fan. The room was set up like a studio apartment, but with more space. There was a small living room, a nearby kitchen, and a Jacuzzi tub, all within sight. The Jacuzzi was on a raised, carpeted platform in a small inset room. It looked to seat four. The two back corners of the room had big, green leafy plants, and there was a skylight above it; a plastic shower curtain adorned with nude Greek statues of men and women, was pulled to the side.

"Nice," I said as my eyes scanned the room.

"Everything you need." Bob said. "I think you'll be very

comfortable. You're welcome to use the Jacuzzi. And, I think there's a few snacks and stuff in the fridge."

"So, I'll sleep on the sofa?" I assumed that it maybe pulled out into a bed.

"No, there's a proper bedroom downstairs," he said walking me over to a door in the back of the room. He switched on another light and we walked down a flight of stairs. The basement was one big, finished bedroom with a Queen-sized bed with a faux-leopard skin comforter, and all the walls were mirrored. Bob went to a nearby closet and pulled the chain for the light bulb.

"There are extra pillows and blankets in here," he directed me to the shelves within. "It stays really cool down here, so you might need an extra blanket."

I walked him back upstairs and to the front door.

"Thanks, Bob. This is really nice." I paused for a moment and then said what I really felt, "You're a really lucky guy."

Not one to accept a compliment, he smiled and joked, "Mom always said I would snatch me a keeper."

And with that, he walked back to the main house where Edward was busy tidying up the patio table and shutting down the house for the evening.

Even though I felt exhausted, the Jacuzzi looked ever so inviting. Certainly I would sleep better after a nice warm soak in the tub. Plus, we had been on the road all day and I needed to hose off the road grime.

It took a moment to size up the situation. The television was within viewing distance of the tub. I could relax in the tub and watch some late-night TV. Using the remote on a nearby coffee table, I pressed the power button and watched the television set illuminate. It was too early to watch David Letterman, my late-night show of preference, however I was able to locate a *M*A*S*H* rerun after pressing the channel selector a few times.

I went to the tub, closed the stopper, and allowed the water to run a bit, waiting for it to get nice and hot. Glancing around, I didn't see any bath oil beads or salts. *Bubbles might be nice*, I thought. I noticed a bottle of dishwashing liquid by the sink. *Eureka!*

Giving the bottle a healthy squeeze, the liquid shot into the tub. I then peeled off my clothes and folded them on a nearby chair. I pressed a button near the tub and the air jets kicked on. The noise was more than I had expected, so I walked over to the remote, a few steps away on a coffee table, turned up the volume on the telly and then turned to return to the tub.

To my utter surprise and horror, the suds in the tub had rapidly ballooned up and they began to spill over onto the floor! There were bubbles, bubbles everywhere!

I raced over to the tub and slapped around the suds, trying to locate the on/off button that had now disappeared in the bubbles. Slap, miss! Slap, miss! And finally, slap! Success! The jets turned off. I could hear the water still running though, which wasn't helping the situation, so I felt around the soapy bubbles for the faucet and the hot and cold water handles. Thankfully, I located them within moments and turned the water off. My heart was racing as I stepped back to assess the situation.

The tub was totally engulfed in white foamy bubbles, two to three feet above the top of the tub, and some of the suds had flowed over unto the thick blue carpeting surrounding the tub and on the floor. *What was I going to do with all of these suds?* I thought. Wasn't this an *I Love Lucy* episode? What would Lucy do?

I looked toward the kitchen and saw a small steel pot on a drying rack near the sink. I grabbed it and used it to bail out suds from the tub and deposit them in the kitchen sink. Luckily, all of the blinds were closed. I couldn't help but think of how ridiculous I must have looked: Butt naked, carrying pots full of soapsuds to the sink, hoping the running water from the kitchen faucet would help dissipate the bubbles.

After a dozen trips, the suds in the tub seemed more manageable, although there was quite a foamy, frothy mess in the kitchen. I was grateful it was a deep, double-sink with a capacity to hold lots of bubbles.

I made a mental note to deal with this mess first thing in the morning, after a good night's rest.

As I stepped into the tub, the warm water felt great, however the bubbles were still providing quite a frothy head to my Jacuzzi latte. I sat down, but couldn't help but laugh to myself; my visibility was minimal as I slowly sank into the foam. On the television, I could hear "Hawkeye" Pierce flirting with Major "Hot Lips" Houlihan, but I could only use my imagination for a visual.

As I soaked in the tub, I couldn't help but realize what a long, long day it had been. To think that we had started at the Cedar City Comfort Inn this morning, visited Zion National Park, stopped over in Las Vegas, survived the desert, dined at the Mad Greek Diner, and now I was relaxing at the Paradise Ranch in Palm Springs in an over-abundance of suds!

Chapter 29

Day Five: And Then, We Rested

After four days of go-go-go, it was a relief to simply sit, stay, and relax during our first full day in Palm Springs. According to my journal entry, it was Wednesday, May 28, 1997.

It must have been early afternoon when I awoke from a short nap. As I eased out of my foggy state, the vibrantly energetic strings of the last movement of Mozart's sublime *Sinfonia Concertante for Violin, Viola and Orchestra in E-flat Major, K.364* gently coaxed me into consciousness. I felt so rested and safe. *Is this heaven?* I thought. I was practically horizontal in a brown leather recliner, with its footrest fully extended so that my feet blocked my view of the pool outside. The patio doors were wide open and an overhead ceiling fan ushered in a warm breeze; no air-conditioning needed. The indoor temperature was the equivalent of a hot August day in Chicago, minus the traditionally oppressive humidity, and yet it felt very pleasant. The scent of chlorine covered my skin, the result of floating about the pool for more than an hour.

My skin was slightly red and hot from the sun, but it was comfortable to the touch. I was wearing a loose-fitting, unbuttoned white gauze shirt, and a pair of dry swimming trunks that were wet when I first sat down. I could feel a thick cotton beach towel underneath me on the chair, there to absorb any remaining dampness from my trunks.

I felt like I was into day two or three of an extensive spa and resort package. My body was at rest. This day wasn't all about relaxation though, as my morning had been quite productive. After a good night's rest, a late breakfast with Bob and Edward, and a quick cleaning session in the kitchen after my *sudsfest,* I had made two phone calls.

The first was to my contact for Bill Maher's *Politically Incorrect* television show, a booking agent named Jackie Miller, who had been involved in a co-promoted event at Harper College with Zanies Comedy Night Club within the past year. My timing was perfect as Maher would be taping in two days at CBS Television City and I'd be on the guest list. I jotted down the details and then called my sister Mary, who lived about an hour west of Palm Springs in Rancho Cucamonga.

Mary had moved to Los Angeles with her husband, also named Michael, back in 1977, a few years after graduating high school. She now worked for a Cadillac dealership and he for Disneyland. We made plans to meet at their home at 3 p.m. the next day and then go to a Quakes game, a Triple-A baseball team for the San Diego Padres franchise. They played at the Rancho Cucamonga ball park called the Epicenter. The Quakes had a mascot named "Tremor" and a baby dinosaur mini-mascot named "After Shock." I loved the tongue-in-cheek humor, which seemed very appropriate since the Epicenter had a statue outside the park of the famous comedian Jack Benny who joked on the radio about a train going to "Azusa and Cuca-monga!" These were two real towns in Southern California with exotic, yet humorous-sounding names. The next couple of days were shaping up nicely.

"Come for a swim?" Edward asked as the three of us finished enjoying our coffee on the terrace. "Swimsuits optional."

It was almost 11 a.m. and the sun was already capable of producing sunburn in a matter of minutes. Sunburn to a man's nether region can be unpleasant bordering on excruciating depending on the severity of the burn, so I kept my swimming trunks on as I dove into the pool.

The water was cool and refreshing as I casually swam the length of the pool using the breaststroke. As I started my return, I turned over on to my back and floated for a while, enjoying the heat of the sun on my face.

Floating. Drifting. Freedom. This experience reminded me of my high school days in the early 1970s, when my friends and I skinny-dipped in a quarry – an abandoned construction site near the outskirts of Elgin, Illinois – tucked away behind thick brush and trees. A friend of mine would drive his old Chevy van — complete with harvest gold shag carpeting covering the entire interior, and an eight-track sound system with free-standing speakers and plenty of cable — down a gravel road and then up to a raised plateau area where we could look out over the crystal clear water and dive off huge ten foot boulders. There'd be four or five of us in the vehicle in early June, maybe days before school let out. Often, we brought big, black inner tube tires to float in. We'd spend hours swimming, floating, and occasionally diving down to view an old refrigerator at the bottom of the quarry some 20 feet below. If we were in a particularly mischievous mood, we brought baseball bats to smash up the rusty, abandoned cars tucked away in the tall grasses and weeds. It was a wonderful release – pure physical therapy — for us teenagers to take a wooden baseball bat and bust up a dilapidated, rusty Chevy or Ford. With luck, we'd get to the vehicle before the windows and headlights were broken and then utterly destroy the virgin glass. As Aerosmith blasted from the van's speaker, we'd sometimes enjoy a joint and celebrate: the day, our youth, and the ultimate feeling of freedom.

A sudden nearby splash jolted me out of my tranquil dream-like memory. Edward had dived in and swam a few laps, while I treaded water near the deep end of the pool, enjoying the warmth of the sun.

Later, I relaxed on an outdoor lounge chair and dried off on a big, thick beach towel, eventually migrating to the indoor leather chair for a nap.

As I woke up, I spied a thick, 600-page paperback English textbook on the nearby coffee table. The title was *Reading and Writing About Short Fiction* by none other than my host, Edward Proffitt. I skimmed the table of contents and noted an impressive collection of more than 80 short stories including those by Chekov, Kafka, Poe, Lawrence, Maupassant, Garcia Marquez, Borges, Beckett, Hemingway and Nabokov; the crème de la crème of the literary set. Edward caught me in the act as he walked in from the pool wrapped in a white terry cloth robe and wearing flip-flops.

"This is a very impressive collection," I said nodding to the book.

"It's a nice intro to writing and fiction," Edward noted nonchalantly. "I really enjoyed compiling the anthology. And, lucky for me, it's popular in academia, so it provides a modest royalty check from time to time." He smiled, letting me know he was more than okay that his effort wasn't totally altruistic. "So, who do you read?"

"Well, let me think. *Siddhartha* by Hermann Hesse is my favorite novel, I must have read it ten times or so. I always seem to get something new from it with each read," I began. I thought a moment about other authors and titles. It was intimidating to cite authors to an English Lit. professor. I couldn't help but think he was judging my selections and sizing me up as a consumer of literature.

"I just finished re-reading Somerset Maugham's *The Razor's Edge*, and I'm a big fan of Hemingway. I like his economical use of words. He can say more in a couple of sentences than most writers do in several pages," I said, sounding like an NPR book reviewer. After hearing myself spout out my list of well-known, mainstream authors, I felt like my taste in literature was conservative and pedestrian at best.

I continued, "I guess I like the modern classics best. I haven't read very many contemporary writers lately. Except maybe for Ian McEwan. I started reading him when I lived in London in 1987 and I think I've read everything he's published since."

"Ah, there's a big literary world out there, Michael," Edward said with a warm professorial smile. "I can make a few recommendations for you, if you'd like. You're in very fine company though, thus far."

"Sure, I'd like that," I said. "I'm always looking for new authors to check out." After a pause, I continued, "Bob says you write poetry. Are you working on anything now?"

"Why, yes I am. Follow me," Edward said as he walked past my chair and into a room in the front of the house that he used as an office. There was a stack of paper in a basket on the desk. Each sheet looked to have a separate poem. "Shall I read for you?"

"I'd like that very much," I said, thrilled that Edward would intimately share his work-in-progress with me.

"These are for a new book, a collection of my poems, that I'm going to call, *Homo Erectus*." He shuffled through a handful of poems, like a blackjack dealer working a deck of cards, looking for just the right poem to act as an introduction to his work. After a moment, he pulled out a paper with just a few lines on it.

"This is a favorite of mine, although it's very short," he said and then paused, allowing for the quiet to establish an air of anticipation.

"It's called, 'Intimacy.' " Another pause.

"As we awake I touch his hand," he began, clearly enunciating each word as he spoke softly and slowly.

"Remembering our passion, now like music heard across a distant shore." Edward's voice trailed off at the end and he gave a hint

of a grin. His cupped right hand waved gently to the side as if he was ushering in a breeze.

It was a beautiful reading and a lovely sentiment. I nodded in approval, "Very nice. One more?"

Edward looked pleased. He pulled out another poem, this one a bit longer.

"This poem has a sense of humor and a bit of a commentary by yours truly."

After another dramatic pause, Edward began, "'Mysterious Ways.'"

He took a breath, and then:

> *"Dr. Laura and the Pope agree;*
> *It's okay to be gay, but not to follow through.*
> *'Hate the sin, but love the sinner,*
> *So they say,*
> *Unless he sins.*
> *Their god is odd,*
> *Creating need*
> *That if fulfilled*
> *Will inexorably propel*
> *Us straight to hell."*

I really liked it, but waited a moment before reacting to allow the final sentence time to linger on my mind.

"Well said," I approved with a nod. "Very clever."

Edward's face reflected a warm glow, appreciation for the compliment.

"And, I want to thank you for all of your hospitality," I continued. "I'm really glad you two met. I've never seen Bob so happy."

"I assure you, the feeling is mutual," Edward said. He placed the papers back on the pile on the desk. "Robert says you fancy yourself a writer as well."

His comment caught me by surprise.

"Well, I've free-lanced a bit here and there for both the *Chicago Tribune* and the *Chicago Sun-Times* as well as smaller publications. A few travel pieces, music reviews; I even covered the Mandela 70th Birthday Tribute show while I was in London. Fun stuff," I said sheepishly. I never know when one's resume starts to sound like bragging, so I proceeded with caution and brevity. "I also wrote an academic book about diversity at the community college level."

"Really?" He looked impressed. "Title?"

I started to laugh, "Something very dry and academic I'm afraid. I was concerned that it would not come up on computer search engines, so it incorporated the words 'student activities,' 'diversity,' and 'community colleges.' So, it's something like, *Diversity, Student Activities and Their Role in Community Colleges*; more practical than catchy and not very exciting, I'm afraid. What is exciting though, is that former Senator Carol Moseley Braun wrote my foreword."

"Smart," Edward grinned. "I'm sure that helped with sales; credibility through affiliation." He slyly added, "Provided your readers approve of politicians, of course."

"Well, it didn't hurt, I guess," I said. "Plus, my book was the first in the field for community colleges; so it filled a void." Since I had a moment alone with Edward, I took advantage of our privacy to share something more intimate. "You know, I'm glad we had a chance to talk.. Bob *really* thinks the world of you. He couldn't get home fast enough."

Edward took a moment to absorb what I had said about Bob. He looked supremely happy, a state of mind the French refer to as *bonheur*.

Edward broke the silence, "Again, I assure you the feeling is mutual. I hope you will enjoy your time here, Michael," he said as he slowly turned to take a seat at his desk. "You'll have to excuse me now for an hour or so. I need to take care of a few phone calls."

"Of course," I said and turned to walk back to the recliner in the other room. Before leaving the room, I noticed a very nicely framed pencil sketch of a young, attractive man, wearing a stiff, white accordion-styled collar; perhaps the subject was a thespian. The artist was very confident, as his lines were flowing and economical, like a rendering by Matisse.

"Nice portrait," I commented. "Who is the artist?"

Edward smiled. "A former lover," he said. "That's actually a portrait of me sketched by a young man I knew many, many years ago." His voice had a warm nostalgic tone, so I knew the picture provoked a fond memory from a previous time in his life.

Like Bob, Edward had been married for many years, and had children, before coming out. It must have been difficult to suppress one's true feelings for years and years, participating in a daily charade to keep up appearances. I was grateful for this time in our society when same-sex partners were becoming more and more accepted in the mainstream, allowing for pride instead of shame. Yet Bob and Edward, as in love and sublimely happy as they appeared, were unable to marry. This fact of American life in the late 1990s was not only unfair, it seemed cruel and unkind. The Paradise Ranch was a safe space for them and their gay friends, a place where they could be who they were without the conditions and guidelines established by a nation perpetually striving for *normal*. And for many Americans in those days, same-sex relationships were not normal. The more I thought about it, *normal* was a setting on a washing machine, or the name for a town in central Illinois; but it was hardly a relevant descriptor for human beings.

"It's a great image," I said to Edward as I prepared to leave his office. "You surround yourself with so much beauty and art. I'm really enjoying my time here. I can see why Bob was so eager to return."

Chapter 30

Closing thoughts

My final afternoon with Bob and Edward at the Paradise Ranch that year, remains vividly burned into my memory to this day.

It was late in the day and we were all sitting poolside. I was lounging on a deck chair in my swimming trunks sipping a cold bottled beer. Bob and Edward were engaged in a lively conversation punctuated with lots of laughter. They were wearing matching purple "Gold's Gym" tank tops with teal lettering, sitting at the outdoor dining table and drinking coffee. Bob and Edward both looked truly happy. At one point, Bob gave Edward a big hug and kissed him on the cheek. With a quick snap of my throwaway camera, I secured one more Kodak Moment.

I thought to myself how I really liked what they had: A committed relationship, with each partner loving the other unconditionally, flaws and all; a goal that — up until that moment — seemed just out of my reach. After years of noncommittal relationships with women, I felt it was time to make progress in my life and find a partner to share our unconditional love as well as a future together. The time had come for me to realize that a leopard was capable of changing his spots; at least this leopard.

In less than 24 hours, I'd be leaving this idyllic retreat and returning to the outside world. For that moment though, I didn't feel any regret for the past or worry about the future. For that moment, I simply focused my senses on enjoying what surrounded me: the warmth of the bright sun; the sound of the classical music playing in the background interrupted ever-so-gently by the fluttering of the nearby palm tree leaves in the light breeze; and the anticipation of a refreshing dip in the cool waters of the swimming pool just inches away. *Life is good* I thought, and even though I had a long journey ahead of me, I closed my eyes and softly laughed at the sun.

Epilogue:

16 Years Later and On the Road Again

I am living proof that a leopard can change his spots! Upon returning from the West Coast, I removed myself from the dating pool for a year and worked on myself as a person and as a potential partner.

I began writing a daily entry in a gratitude diary, expressing my sincere thanks for all the blessings I had taken for granted. I wasn't a regular viewer of *The Oprah Winfrey Show*, however I had an uncanny ability to catch episodes that would eventually impact my life. This was the case with keeping a gratitude diary.

Then with the help of a good friend who was a member of Alcoholics Anonymous, I created a modified 12-step program designed to help me address both my co-dependency and commitment-phobic issues. Between these two efforts, I gradually learned to: appreciate what I had; love myself; and make amends with those I had thoughtlessly hurt (or at least attempt to make amends, not everyone was keen on forgiving my love-related blunders).

During this time, as I approached several former romantic partners – survivors of my bungled relationships – I harvested "love lessons" so that I could learn from my mistakes.

If I had failed to purchase appropriate romantic presents (read: Jewelry) in a past relationship, I made a note for future reference. If I had been insensitive during discussions with a former partner, I learned how to better handle the situation and recorded the results in my journal (*"Oops, I'm sorry. I obviously offended you. Please tell me how I could have handled that better."*). And, above all, *if* I was fortunate enough to find someone who met my criteria for a life partner, I promised myself that I wouldn't hesitate to make a commitment to her. No more waiting several years to let the person know that I wanted to be with her for the long-term.

As for my criteria, I determined that the *ideal person* for me would: 1) be happy from within (she would be positive and enthusiastic about life); 2) be attractive to me and take good care of herself (she would exercise and not abuse alcohol, drugs, and food); and most importantly, 3) she would love me for who I am (my Brass Ring: *Unconditional love*). Secondary concerns included that she would: be loving and passionate; appreciate culture, music, art, travel and nature; and be financially responsible (not a Super Consumer).

As for me, to attract such a person, I knew I needed to be nurturing, giving (without concern for reciprocation), positive, enthusiastic about life, and accepting of the other person. I truly needed to give unconditional love in return.

After a year, I permitted myself to slowly ease back into dating, approaching women more carefully, making sure a potential partner: didn't have a bad relationship with her father; was available and interested in a long-term commitment; and was a good match for me (no more having sex for sex sake!).

Somewhere along the way, I had heard that "you attract who you feel you deserve." Since I was feeling better about myself I looked for individuals who were solid potential partners.

I dated a few people and was more present in the relationships, however I struggled with finding partners who didn't have significant concerns within their histories. One woman was a single mom and I greatly appreciated her and her child, but her ex-husband was a real problem and someone I didn't want to have in my life.

Another woman was in deep financial debt and kept that a secret from me. In fact, I caught her in a series of lies, which was obviously not the foundation for a good relationship.

After striking out several times, I found myself in a relationship slump and wondered what I could do to meet new people. As an extra incentive to motivate myself to seek out new potential partners, I bought concert tickets for a period of three months, one show per month, which included three of my favorite performers: Sting, David Bowie, and Joe Cocker. I had great seats for the three shows and each had sold out, so they were definitely *hot* events. Unfortunately for me, I was unable to identify a potential romantic partner to accompany me to any of the shows. As it turned out, I treated close female friends to join me (by the way, I also considered my close female friends as potential romantic partners — a la *When Harry Met Sally* — however, crossing over from friend to lover was extremely awkward and problematic in each of these cases).

After months of trying to meet the right person, I came to terms with my situation. I had: a loving, caring family; several dear friends who love me and are also single; a great job; and been able to travel to exotic destinations whenever I wanted. Life was good, and if I didn't have a partner, then I needed to be okay with my situation; and I was! It was November 2004 when I came to this conclusion, and I booked a trip for myself to China and Tibet for the following April.

In March 2005 while scraping wallpaper for several hours in a condo I had recently purchased, I found myself in dire need of a good, strong cup of coffee to keep me going, so I walked over to my favorite nearby coffee shop and bakery. It was afternoon and not the usual time I would have been there for a coffee break. As I was adding milk and sugar to my coffee at the service island, I spied a familiar face at a nearby table. She was a former student I had known 16 years earlier at Harper College. I'm not usually very good at remembering names, but in this case, it came to me right away: Laura!

She was speaking with another woman and I hesitated interrupting them, but she had looked my way and our eyes locked. I had no choice but to walk over and say "hi." Unknown to me at the time is that I was about to say something to her that I had never said to a woman before.

"Laura?," I said somewhat timidly, but with a smile. She acknowledged that I was correct and said my name. She remembered me! Laura had always been very attractive, so I could only assume she was involved in a relationship. Therefore, I awkwardly blurted out my next line, "So, how are you? You must be married, right?"

How lame! I thought. *What a horrible opening line!*

She chuckled and looked at the woman, then back at me.

"No, I'm not married. I travel a lot."

"So do I!" My eyes lit up and I saw an opportunity to strike up a conversation with her.

I learned that the woman was her mother, Diane, and that Laura was teaching Spanish at a high school in nearby Skokie, Illinois. I was so nervous that I didn't make a mental note about her place of employment, and feeling like I was intruding, I said it was really great to see her, said goodbye, and walked away to a nearby table to enjoy my coffee.

Her phone number! I didn't get it! I tried to make eye contact with her again, but the chance never came up and she soon left with her mom.

Lucky for me, the next day, I tracked down her school e-mail address using Google and then I sent her a note.

We went on a coffee date the following weekend, and I asked her to marry me nine months later; and we were married in Maui nine months after that. As I write this book, we've been very happily married for more than eight years!

In retrospect, I can't help but consider the road trip that Bob and I took in 1997 as somewhat of a *Hero's Journey* for me, a chance for me to embark on self-awareness, adventure, and change.

As for Bob and Edward, they continued their close, idyllic relationship traveling the world and sharing exotic adventures in places such as Bali, Bhutan, Easter Island, the Amazon, Antarctica, and Australia. They were joined together in a civil union in 2003, and later legally married in July 2008, several months before *Proposition 8*.

Desiring a more culturally interesting environment to live in, they left Palm Springs for the San Francisco Bay Area, and found a beautiful home in Oakland, not far from Berkeley, and moved in March 2009.

Bob remained with Edward until Edward's death from liver cancer in March 2012. I'm grateful to have spent time with Edward before his passing when I visited them in January of the same year.

Although in excruciating pain and his senses somewhat dulled by the medical marijuana he took to manage the pain, Edward was his usual kind and generous self, expounding on the topics of the day, thrashing Republican ultra-conservatism while managing his wealth and making fiscal preparations for Bob. Edward may not have been a saint, and Bob had certainly shared his alcohol-related indiscretions with me over the years, however this was a side of Edward I had very little exposure to and had not experienced first-hand. To me, Edward was a fascinating character who was fiscally conservative, yet socially liberal, a great conversationalist and a poet until his dying day.

Later that same year, I retired from Harper College and began pulling together old journals and notes to write this book. In November 2012, I began writing the book in earnest, not really sharing this information with anyone outside of Laura.

Two months later, while on the phone with Bob, he asked me if I'd like to go on another road trip, this time from Chicago to San Francisco via the American Southwest. I was shocked to hear him ask me about a road trip completely out-of-the-blue.

"You'll never believe what I'm up to these days," I said coyly, and then I filled him in on my goal to write this book.

Over the next few weeks, we compiled an itinerary that included: a music-oriented adventure in Branson, Missouri; a stop in Glen Rose, Texas to visit the Creation Evidence Museum (we were curious to see how the proprietors proved that dinosaurs and humans inhabited the Earth at the same time); a drive south to Austin to witness the Cathedral of Junk; then head way north in Texas for the Cadillac Ranch near Amarillo; and then, we'd venture over to The UFO Capital of the U.S., Roswell, New Mexico. I playfully named our proposed 2013 road-less-travelled trip the "Odyssey of Oddities" and began developing the ultimate music mix for such an offbeat adventure.

Bob was planning to come to Chicago in early May to visit his mother, Millie, as a Mother's Day gift. Our plan was to then leave Chicago on Sunday, May 12, spend eight to nine days on the road, and then I'd fly home from San Francisco on Tuesday, May 21. So, I purchased a one-way ticket from San Francisco to Chicago about six weeks before the trip.

As the trip drew near though, Bob began to feel anxious and depressed as he was still coping with losing Edward and dealing with the harsh reality that for the first time in his life, he was living alone. In mid-April I received a call from Bob and he explained that he wasn't up for the trip; it was canceled. I was disappointed, but understood the situation. A few days later, he suggested that, since I already had a one-way ticket home, he'd pay for my flight to San Francisco. He proposed that we go on a series of mini-road trips for a week or so, to Yosemite National Park, then to Big Sur and Monterey, and later maybe to Napa Valley. I was elated! We wouldn't have a chance to drive cross-country, however a week of experiencing some of Northern California's finest tourist attractions was a fine compromise.

As I flew to San Francisco, I couldn't help but think of how our situations had dramatically changed since our last road trip in 1997. Currently, I was in a happy, committed relationship and Bob was newly single and going through a significant change in his life. This was a 180-degree shift from where we were some 16 years earlier.

Once settled at the Casa de Fischer in Oakland, I learned that Bob was in the midst of compiling portraits of Bay Area poets and writers for a proposed book. His friend and colleague, Charles, arranged the sessions and I tagged along to a couple of his photo shoots.

I was eager to return to Yosemite, where I had been twice before, for a Muir-like photo excursion and to re-connect with nature at its finest. However, I patiently allowed my host to complete his business-at-hand.

After three days, almost the mid-point of my vacation, I pressed the issue. Bob felt emotionally overwhelmed and not up to the trip to Yosemite, but offered a day excursion to Carmel and Big Sur. I had never been to either, so I was happy to experience a new adventure with my buddy. Immediately, I imagined an idyllic afternoon of sun, sand and surf, walking along the ocean, viewing whales and sea lions, and perhaps, sipping a cocktail from the deck of a quaint waterside restaurant. The excursion I had in mind would certainly make this trip to Oakland worthwhile and most likely become one of the highlights of my year.

On Saturday, May 18, we got up just before sunrise and pointed Bob's Mini-Cooper southeast down Route 880 toward San Jose, and eventually to Route 1 and onward to Monterey, Carmel and Big Sur.

Of course, I came prepared with a "Road Trip 2013" mix-CD that I had specifically burned for this adventure. The CD showcased a fine selection of road-worthy tunes by artists including Tame Impala, The Wallflowers, Bob Mould, Los

Lobos, Jack White, White Stripes, Dave Matthews, Tom Petty, Aerosmith, the Rolling Stones, and ZZ Ward. I popped the CD into his player and the thumping, gritty, stripped-down Blues of Pat MacDonald, formerly of Timbuk 3, began to fill the air. The first two-cuts, "Blues of Sin/BabyLove" and "Drinkin' Or Drivin'," were from his new album *Purgatory Hill* and featured some fine slide guitar and his easily identifiable vocals.

Ah, the open road, cool music, and my buddy behind the wheel, I thought. I was starting to feel really excited and happy. This was the escape I had longed for! We were on a quest for kicks and adventure on the West Coast. What could be better?

"Can we listen to something a little more....quieter?" Bob inquired with a slight whine in his voice. If I didn't know better, his reaction reminded me of someone recovering from a nasty hangover and in need of some soft, tranquil Muzak.

Obviously, it was too early for such raucous rock, I thought. Hell, the sun had only gotten up a few moments ago. *Understandable*, I thought and clicked down the playlist to a more laid-back "Burn It Down" by Los Lobos and "Rooftop" by the Dave Matthews Band. After a few more minutes, Bob asked for some quiet. Absolute quiet.

"Oh, okay," was my barely audible response. I was disappointed, but it was early, so that was okay.

"I have a few questions to ask you to fact-check some points in my book. Do you mind if I spend some time interviewing you?"

Bob was happy to comply. So from my small black backpack, I pulled out a leather-bound notebook, with "Carpe Diem" etched on the front, and started asking Bob a series of questions. I had accumulated roughly a dozen questions over the past few months about Bob's personal history, and I needed exact dates or clarification to make sure my memory was accurate, or at least close.

We were driving past Fremont on Route 880, the speedometer fluctuating between 75 and 80 mph, when I asked Bob to confirm a timeline I had developed about when he met

Edward and when they moved in together. As I was jotting down a few notes, I heard a tremendous thump on my side of the car. It startled me and my head jolted up out of my journal. The day before, I had noticed that the front tire on the car's passenger side seemed a bit low, so my first thought was that it was a blow out. Bob continued driving, barely slowing down. He looked pale and startled.

"What was that?"

Bob didn't respond.

"Maybe we should pull over," I said as I tried to determine what had just happened. My first thought of a blow out was not feasible as we continued down the road without even a hint of the dramatic rhythmic thumping of a flat tire.

Bob complied with my request, turning on his right turn signal and slowly shifting from the inner, fast lane of the three-lane highway, to the shoulder of the road.

"I hit Bambi," Bob declared as we came to a stop. I think he had suddenly awoken from being in a state of shock.

I got out of the car and inspected the front end. I could see significant damage to the front panel on the passenger side of the car. Much of the panel was gone and there were patches of fur and what appeared to be deer feces on the fender and hood. I looked back down the road at least 200 yards but couldn't see any deer carcass. My first thought was that it was injured and ran into the nearby woods. Two cars had pulled off the road immediately behind us and their drivers were rushing out to assist us.

"You okay?" A tall man asked us. "I've seen accidents like this before and you two are *damn* lucky to walk away alive!"

The second driver, a middle-aged guy with an Oakland Raiders baseball cap, made a similar remark.

Bob looked a little shaken but his first words confirmed he was still the same Bob, "We should find the deer and take it with us. I love venison!"

The tall gentleman, who introduced himself as Jim, suggested that we locate the deer and take a photo as proof for auto insurance purposes.

Great idea, I thought as I grabbed my small point-and-shoot camera and the two of us hiked back toward the overpass where Jim said he saw the deer. It was a good 400 yards away from the car. As Jim and I began walking, Bob called for road service and the police.

Jim was really very kind to keep me company as we walked back to the deer. Although he meant well, he kept reiterating that we were really lucky to not have been seriously injured or killed. That kind of information really freaked me out. I silently said a prayer thanking God for watching over us that morning.

As we walked down the road, Jim said that it was really odd how the deer, a smaller doe, had come from the housing complex on the east side of the road, crossed the three lanes, hopping a four-foot high barrier and into our lane of traffic. It was heading *toward* a forest. Usually, one would expect seeing wildlife coming from the forest, not from a housing development.

After walking approximately 350 yards, we saw the deer remains on the shoulder of the road. As we got closer, I took several pictures to show its close proximity to the road. Once upon the furry victim, I took a variety of shots, not unlike a police photographer at a crime scene. It was depressing to see such a beautiful animal lying there dead; its dark eyes foggy and blood streaming from its nose.

Jim and I headed back to Bob's car and I thanked him for all of his help. Bob had called the police and we waited a brief ten minutes for a state trooper to report the accident for Bob's impending insurance claim.

The trooper assessed the situation quickly and told us that, if the car was drivable, to take it to the nearest gas station. The dealership where Bob had purchased the car was only minutes down the road in Fremont, so we decided to take the car there for repair.

I complimented Bob on his driving as he certainly had avoided a potentially fatal accident.

"I barely had time to react," he admitted. "I saw the deer come from the corner of my eye. There wasn't time to change lanes, so I decided to grab hold of the wheel and drive through the animal. I knew I wouldn't hit him straight on. I must have just clipped him."

"Thank goodness you didn't hit him head on, or he'd have been in our laps!"

The thought made me grimace. We were certainly lucky.

We drove south about a half a mile to the next junction where we could turn around.

As we turned off the road, crossed the overpass, and then returned to 880 now going northeast, I figured the road trip to Carmel/Big Sur was over. Instead of a peaceful, serene day on the coast enjoying the sun and surf, we'd most likely spend the next few hours dealing with an auto shop and then heading home. I was bummed.

"We can get a car rental from the dealership and at least get to Carmel for lunch," Bob said matter-of-factly.

I couldn't believe Bob would still want to continue our quest after such a traumatic incident. My attitude shifted from sad to glad and I let out a big smile.

"That's very cool, Bob. I'll treat to a really great lunch. We need to celebrate our surviving this morning."

"Well, I know this trip is important to you and I haven't exactly been the best travel partner this week," he admitted.

Our time at the auto dealership was remarkably short. Bob had called ahead while I was taking portraits of the departed doe, so they had a rental car washed and ready for us. After signing some paperwork, we pulled our personal possessions out of Bob's Mini-Cooper and transferred them to our rental car, a little Toyota Yaris, a car name that I believe stems from a goddess in Greek mythology named Charis, who was a symbol for cramped quarters and tinny construction.

After eating a full breakfast at a nearby diner, we returned to Route 880 and our destination of Carmel (I wondered if it was once named Caramel and then truncated by uncouth tourists?). It was only 10:30 a.m., so Bob felt confident that we'd arrive in time for lunch. Since we were on the road again, I suggested we pop in the CD and turn up some tunes.

This time Bob selected the music, and after the partial destruction of his Mini-Cooper, a car that was less than a year old, who was I to complain. Bob inserted a CD into the player, and we listened to a Swing version of *The Mikado*, recorded in the 1950s. Bob certainly had an offbeat, eclectic taste in music, and even though I'm pretty open to any type of musical genre, this one would be challenging for me to appreciate beyond the first few minutes.

It was a Saturday and our morning's worth of delays meant that we'd hit significant traffic congestion the closer we came to our coastal destination, as it's mandatory for all Californians to spend every clear, sunny weekend at the beach. I think it's a state law.

Eventually, we made our way to Route 1, which parallels the ocean. Going south on Route 1, heading toward Monterey and Carmel, I noticed a distinct division the highway created between the beauty and majesty of the ocean and dunes to the west, and to the east, rampant commercialism with a prolonged strip mall hogging the countryside with familiar logos for Target, Staples, and Kohl's, among others, forming a cluttered skyline.

Bob liked to drive fast and he had great confidence in his brakes, far more than I. While we were driving the safe, smooth-handling Mini-Cooper, I felt secure with his Grand Prix-like antics. But our car was now a fucking Yaris, which handled like a tin can on wheels, so I was more than a bit concerned, bordering on frightened. In fact, I pressed an imaginary brake pedal multiple times on my passenger side and held my breath as Bob weaved through traffic, accelerating past a variety of cars and trucks. For once, I wished there was a governor on the carburetor.

We arrived at Carmel-by-the-Sea at 12:30 p.m. and although the downtown area was very crowded, we were able to snag a prime parking space near a park where an outdoor art fair was being held. The Parking Gods favored our quest!

Although we were fairly close to the ocean, it was not prominently in view. I could just barely make it out beyond the trees at the end of the street we were on. The downtown area was made up of a blocks upon blocks of quaint boutique shops, restaurants and galleries, with advertisements for wine-tastings every ten feet or so. The sidewalks were filled with tourists. By weird coincidence, the first gallery Bob and I entered featured a stylized, metal deer, about the size of the one we had just hit. We took it as a sign. Carmel was not the experience we needed this day; it was not what I had imagined, and therefore, not part of our quest.

We retrieved the car and got back on the road, next stop Big Sur. The open road was now more inviting, as there were no signs of man, other than the paved road. There were hills to the east and the ocean to the west. I was getting pretty hungry, but we saw no sign of any upcoming restaurants, taverns or little towns for that matter. I would have to be patient and wait until we arrived at Big Sur, some 25 miles down the road.

About 10 minutes had passed when Bob suddenly braked hard and made an extreme right into a driveway that was barely visible.

"Ed and I were here before," he said with glee, following a gravel road by a tall green hedge. "This is a really good restaurant and it has an incredible view of the ocean!"

I caught my breath, for a moment I thought his abrupt maneuver had involved dodging another deer.

We had turned into Rocky Point, a restaurant serving "California Coastal Cuisine with a European Flare." It was a nice enough looking eatery, but it was the view that made this THE culinary stop between Monterey and Big Sur. There was an extensive wooden deck that looked out over the ocean and the rocky coast below. It was now after 1 p.m., the place was crowded and we didn't have a reservation. Seating was available both indoors and out. We held our breath and hoped for outdoor seating.

"Two for lunch, please," I said to the hostess at the entry of the dining room. Bob walked a few steps ahead of me, his bright purple hair catching the attention of many of the diners. Like an impatient child, Bob poked his head into the room, looking for open tables and checking out the beautiful view.

The hostess took two menus and said to follow her. She walked through the dining room and then out to the deck. It was windy, but the view was amazing. We continued to follow her down a flight of stairs and into a private grotto-like seating area. This protected seating area not only blocked the wind, but we had a divine, unobstructed view of the ocean. It was absolutely perfect!

Bob and I proceeded to have several glasses of wine, Carmel Road Pinot Noir, my favorite at the time, followed by an amazing seafood lunch and a rhubarb and strawberry crumble cake for dessert, along with a couple of flawless cappuccinos. Although the day had begun with a life-threatening accident, it was now providing us with a blissful experience that reminded us that our lives were really wonderful.

As we sipped our wine, I looked out at the horizon and saw a spray of water. After a few moments, several yards further south, I saw another spray of water. It was a whale! I confirmed this with a local diner at a nearby table.

"How cool is that," I declared, always in awe of nature. "Life is good."

As we sat there, bathing in the warmth of the sun and enjoying the sound of the waves hitting the nearby rocks, I couldn't help but think of how things had really worked out for the best.

If we had driven across the country, we would have been miserable. Texas was so big, flat and hot that time of year. We would have been in a cramped car with two very opposing opinions on the definition of "good music." Surely, we would have come close to blows and I doubt we would have had a very good time. Besides, physically I couldn't tolerate long drives. My back was already stiff over the short venture we had that day, let alone driving seven days and thousands of miles. We weren't able to relive the trip we had taken 16 years earlier, and that was okay. Bob and I were in different places in our lives and it was really nice just to spend some quality time together.

"To good wine, good food, and good friends," I said, lifting my glass in a toast to Bob.

"Good friends," he echoed as we clinked glasses, a rare sentimental gesture. Then, with barely a beat, he returned to form, "You know, I'm in a pretty good place considering Bambi almost fucked up our day."

With that, we sipped our wine, looked out at the sun and laughed.

ABOUT THE AUTHOR

Michael Nejman is always in hot pursuit of *The Holy Grail of Guilty Pleasures & Heavenly Delights,* although it tends to constantly change as he expands his list of blissful experiences. A few of his current guilty pleasures include: The Stanley Hotel's (Estes Park, CO) Root Beer Float, made up of vanilla bean gelato and Barq's Root Beer; Ho Hos (especially frozen); Tom & Wendee's Italian Ice (Chicago, IL) which has an amazing chocolate-flavored ice that he loves with the black cherry ice; salted caramel-flavored macaroons from Guard and Grace (Denver, CO) carrot cake cupcakes from Sweet C's Bakery (Palatine, IL); and fresh blueberries that are in-season.

Likes: The Rolling Stones; *Siddhartha* by Hermann Hesse; *Casablanca; It's a Wonderful Life; The Shawshank Redemption; Almost Famous; The New York Times'* Sunday edition; *Entertainment Weekly;* CBS *Sunday Morning;* WBEZ's *Sound Opinions* podcast; WXRT 93.1FM; Virgin Airlines; Beck; Stevie Wonder; David Letterman; Jon Stewart; Amy Schumer; *Broad City;* travel to exotic locations; discovering cool cemeteries; *Groundhog Day; True Romance; Pulp Fiction;* and *Green Acres.*

Dislikes: Coach seats on most airlines, as they are the nearest thing to legalized torture in our country (Virgin Airlines is the exception); Citizens United; and our nation's inability to: provide universal health care, adopt common sense gun control laws, provide campaign finance reform, and overcome partisan politics (compromise is better than an utter lack of progress).

For more information about the author, please visit:
www.michaelnejman.com

CPSIA information can be obtained
at www.ICGtesting.com
Printed in the USA
LVOW04s1327290216

477144LV00026B/493/P